CREATE.
CONNECT.
CONVERT.

25 LESSONS ON HOW TO OWN YOUR VALUE
& BUILD A POWERFUL PROFESSIONAL
PRESENCE USING SOCIAL MEDIA
(WITHOUT BRAGGING).

LESLIE HUGHES

TORONTO, ONTARIO

Publisher Production Solutions | PPS Publishing
3-1750 The Queensway Suite 1312
Toronto ON M9C 5H5
www.ppspublishing.com
Ordering Information: quantity sales are available on quantity purchases by corporations, associations, and others. For details, contact the publisher at the address above.

Paperback ISBN: 978-0-9936905-9-4
eBook ISBN: 978-0-9952750-0-3
10 9 8 7 6 5 4 3 2 1

Library and Archives Canada Cataloguing in Publication

Hughes, Leslie, 1970-, author
Create. Connect. Hughes, Leslie, 1970-, author
Create. Connect. Convert : 25 lessons on how to own your value &
build a powerful professional presence using social media (without bragging)
/ Leslie Hughes.

Issued in print and electronic formats.
ISBN 978-0-9936905-7-0 (paperback).--ISBN 978-0-9936905-8-7 (html)

1. Internet marketing. 2. Branding (Marketing). 3. Social media.
I. Title.

HF5415.1265.H845 2016   658.8'72   C2016-906307-0
                                                  C2016-906308-9

Printed and Published in Canada

Cover Photo Copyright © 2016 by Rebecca Tisdelle-Macias
Cover design by Rob Ciancamerla
Book Design by Doris Chung

TABLE OF CONTENTS

FORWARD

"...A brain, trapped in the body of a game show hostess."

Say Anything

Like a Trojan Horse, this book is a strategy, but it's wrapped in the body of how to feel confident about telling your professional brand story.

Let me tell you, owning my value hasn't always come easy.

Despite having over 20 years of marketing and sales experience, including 10+ years of digital marketing/social media experience, I often felt (and still struggle with the feeling) that I wasn't "enough."

Sure, I know a lot about marketing; I read and watch and listen to marketing ALL. THE. TIME. I consume VAST amounts of information so I can stay on top of an ever-changing industry.

I had a huge "a-ha!" when I heard (and met!) author and social media aficionado/expert Gary Vaynerchuk at The Art of Marketing in Toronto. During his speech, he said the following (paraphrased):

"You probably know just as much about social media as I do. The only difference between you and me, is that I have the guts to stand up here and talk about it."

When I heard Gary say this, I realized that I probably *could* do what he does. I had already worked with well-recognized brands helping them develop social media strategies. I had been teaching college students about social media for over five years, and providing instruction for the Social Media Marketing Certificate at The University of Ontario

Institute of Technology. I knew a lot of the information he was sharing in his keynote presentations; I just needed to get out of my own way.

It wasn't until I read both *Lean In* by Sheryl Sandberg, and *Bossypants* by (my idol) Tina Fey where they each admitted they, too, had moments when they felt like they weren't enough to be in charge of leading a team. Just like everyone else, they also have fears: fear of not being liked, fear of making the wrong decision, and fear of failure.

If these intelligent, talented, and successful women are raising their hands to admit "me too", and *they* are being vulnerable enough to admit it in print, then we are all in this struggle together!

It's almost impossible for you to see how amazing you are. You will never be able to see yourself how others see you. I'm sure other people have complimented you, and instead of accepting this praise, the little voice in your head says, "that's just crazy talk!"

The reason I began writing this book is because I've realized that everyone, from the shopkeeper on Main Street to the executives on Wall Street feel the same way: challenged to own their value. I write and optimize LinkedIn profiles for senior executives in Canada and the U.S., and I have been quite surprised to learn that some of them feel very uncomfortable speaking about their "wins" and accomplishments. I hear them say things like:

- "I don't want to brag."
- "I don't really like to be in the spotlight."
- "I was only a part of a team that accomplished the big project."

We've all been taught to be modest and not to boast, which is a good thing, because no one can stand a pompous ass. At the same time, I know what holds many people back from owning their value is the feeling that they are unworthy of their accomplishments or recognition.

We all universally fear rejection and we all want to be accepted. It's normal to want to avoid pain and gravitate towards pleasure.

So let me make one thing abundantly clear:

You are enough.
Wherever you are on your
journey to success is exactly
where you're supposed to be.

By the end of this book, I hope you feel empowered. I hope you realize, as Glinda the Good Witch told Dorothy:

"Everything you were looking for was right there with you all along."

The journey to success isn't always easy. It's definitely a moving target. It's not the grand gestures that will suddenly transform your life; it's the small micro-changes that add up to big changes over time.

You probably will never recognize the moment you've "made it". You may never actually see the way you look from the viewpoint of your target audience.

But, in all your imperfections, and with all of your experience and perspective, *you are perfect.* You alone are responsible for owning your value. You can't get it from a bottle or a pill. There is no silver bullet. No one else can make you feel strong and "complete."

Make a commitment to yourself, right now, that you'll complete the enclosed exercises. Invest in you.

Together, we'll create your professional brand, and leverage social media to create a strong presence, connect with quality people, and convert higher-paying clients. When you step into your value and own your worth, success will follow.

Now let's help you get out of your way!

Best,

Leslie

@punchmediadotca

P.S. *"Nothing is impossible, the word itself says 'I'm possible'!"*—Audrey Hepburn.

INTRODUCTION

This book is *not* for you if you expect the changes to happen *without* putting in any effort.

Nothing happens by osmosis. You have to complete *all* the exercises to produce optimum results.

This book *is* for you if you're a professional who is looking to:

- feel powerful and confident about your online presence,
- access the easiest ways to craft your compelling brand story,
- learn the proper "netiquette" to make quality connections,
- understand the triggers to get people to invest in what you're doing/selling,
- deepen relationships and keep your business relationships happy.

This book is part storytelling, part lessons, and part workbook. You'll be able to apply these strategies whether you're an entrepreneur, work for a large corporation, or looking for new business opportunities. If you are a professional who is looking to develop your career by marketing yourself as a thought leader, then this book is for you.

Now is the time for you to take action Not tomorrow. Not next week.
Not when _____(insert your excuse here) happens.

"The best time to plant a tree is 20 years ago. The second best time is now."

~Chinese Proverb

"If you don't take action, you won't gain traction."

~Leslie Hughes (yes, I'm quoting myself.)

"Just do it."

~NIKE

I was involved in digital marketing for almost 20 years (where did the time go?!). I've worked with some amazing brands to develop their online presence.

Now, I'm ready to help *you*: the brand.

Together we'll develop your personalized brand strategy, using LinkedIn as the primary social media channel. LinkedIn is the world's largest professional networking site, and in my opinion, the most powerful channel for your brand. I'll admit, it's not the "sexy" channel where people gleefully shout "woohoo!" when they log in, but members who are using LinkedIn for professional networking understand that it isn't the site where you waste time: it's the site where you invest time.

In this book, there are anecdotes, lessons, and action items. We won't be going through a deep dive with all the "how-to's", but we will cover the essential elements that you can focus on to maximize your results. I've even included some cool worksheets and "swipe files" to make the process that much easier! (You're welcome!)

In Module #1, we will work toward creating your brand and get a clear picture of your story. I'll shed light on some of my own fears, frustrations and "a-ha" moments and you'll learn how to reframe your fear. We'll also spend time getting into the mindset of your ideal target audience so that you can speak to them in their "language" and exceed their expectations. In Module #2, we move on to cover the various ways you can connect with people online using the right (n)etiquette, and why you shouldn't connect with everyone. In Module #3, we will wrap up with the top ways you can dominate your niche as a thought leader, "convert" your audience, and empower your "raving fans" to become your unpaid sales team!

I may not have met you yet, but I believe in you. I believe that you were put on this earth for a purpose. You have an expertise in something *no* one else has.

We are both lucky to have been born in a time where we are not limited to depending upon mass media to share our knowledge.

As long as you're taking action, I'm with you on this journey — every step of the way.

MY STORY

When I was little, I always wanted to be "the smart one". I wanted to be Sabrina in *Charlie's Angels*. I felt much more connected to Janet on *Three's Company* than I did with the air-headed Chrissy. When my best friend and I would chat about growing up and living together like *Laverne and Shirley*, I felt I was much more Shirley than Laverne.

I was never the rebel or the sassy one.

I was (and still am) a book nerd *and* a chatterbox, a total ambivert (both an extrovert and an introvert). To quote Donny and Marie, *"I'm a little bit country and a little bit rock & roll."*

When I was a kid, I would get into a lot of trouble for talking too much in class. Even when the teachers would put me next to the quietest kid, I'd find a way to keep nattering on. (Look at me now, teachers! I get paid to speak for a living!)

I love to connect with people, and yet I also love to isolate myself so that I can create content and consume as much knowledge as possible.

I've always been fascinated with the "why" behind what people think and do. I majored in Psychology at University and obtained both my Practitioner's and Master Practitioner's Certificate in Neurolinguistic Programming (NLP). (If you're familiar with Tony Robbins, he uses NLP in a lot of his work.)

I think that's why I love marketing so much: it involves various principles of psychology and sociology to (benevolently) manipulate people to buy products or services.

Even as a chatty girl, public speaking hasn't always come naturally to me. Speaking in front of people (particularly strangers) used to make me feel weak in the knees, and I thought everyone could see how much I was shaking inside.

I've realized that sometimes how we feel on the inside is completely different than the perception others have of us.

I also found that taking my NLP Practitioner's course with Elizabeth Payea-Butler opened up my eyes (and ears!) to the power of our subconscious and the subtle ways we can use language for good. The presuppositions for NLP are good principles for life. These principles have helped me see that opportunities are found on the other side of obstacles.

Some NLP presuppositions include:

- There is no failure, only feedback. You have all the resources you need.
- Every behavior has a positive intention.
- People make the best choice they can at the time.
- The person or element with the most flexibility in a system will have the most influence.
- Modeling successful performance leads to excellence.
- We process all information through our senses.
- If what you are doing isn't working, do something else.

I've realized that when I allow my conscious, constructive brain to go quiet, I then focus on providing valuable content. And when I focus on being "of service," then I enjoy the process and the audience is much more receptive to the messages as well.

There's no better way of explaining it, but I overcame my fear of public speaking because "I got out of my way."

Don't get me wrong. I still get nervous in new situations.

I reached out to a producer at CTV and expressed my interest in appearing as a guest on *The Social*. When they said "yes," and I realized I was going to be on live television in front of thousands of people, I panicked a little. I had a few sleepless nights, and on the day of the event, I realized that showing my fear on camera wasn't going to be good for me, for the audience, or for the show. So I simply "let it go." I was still nervous, but I was also excited. And the second I finished the segment, I was exhilarated and couldn't wait to do it again!

I love teaching. I love presenting. I really love helping people simplify the complex world of social media so it makes sense to them.

But enough about me. Let's talk about you.

I want you to start thinking: what do you love to do? What makes you passionate? What makes your soul *sing*?

Combine your passion with what you're good at, and *this* is where you find the "sweet spot."

Remember: no one knows what *you* know from *your* perspective.

It's time for you to stand in your value.

As Dr. Seuss says:

"Today you are you, that is truer than true. There is no one alive that is youer than you."

So let's get started, shall we?

MODULE #1

CREATE

The question isn't "what are we going to do," the question is "what aren't we going to do?"

~Ferris Bueller Day Off

Have you ever thought of yourself as a brand?

Your mom probably always told you "you're special" and "you're unique," but the truth is – you really *are*!

No one knows what *you* know from *your* perspective. You bring value to the universe. You are an expert.

Did you know that the origin of the word "brand" meant "burn," and in the 1500s, the word was used to describe how people would mark their property?

It makes sense that the word brand used in marketing and advertising would essentially mean "to leave a mark or impression."

You leave an impression with each and every person you connect with. Have you ever thought about what people think about your brand?

Take a moment to think of your favorite celebrity. Maybe it's Beyoncé, George Clooney, or David Beckham. Do you think of them as people, or as a brand? What immediately comes to mind when you think of this famous person?

YOU DON'T NEED TO BE FAMOUS TO BE A BRAND.

Thanks to tools such as blogging, YouTube, Twitter, and LinkedIn, **we are *all* media agencies**, and we all have easily-accessible and affordable platforms to reach people around the world.

These channels are collectively called "social media," and the Social Media Revolution is arguably the biggest shift since the Industrial Revolution.

In traditional media, we have long depended on newspapers, TV, radio, magazines, etc. to disseminate content to the masses. This form of communication is *pushed* one-way: from the medium to the audience. For the most part, only large organizations can afford to hire a team to design and execute campaigns. Their goal? To gain market share and earn more profits by persuading their audience to buy their stuff.

Traditional marketing (typically advertising) is designed to interrupt the audience while their attention is focused on the content or experience. For example, when we watch TV, listen to the radio, or read a magazine, the commercial or ad is designed to interrupt our experience by screaming for your attention. Essentially, they are waving their jazz hands and (metaphorically) screaming *"Look at me!! Listen to my message!!"*

I used to sell advertising for Weddingbells and FASHION Magazine. I would explain to my clients that the success of their campaign would be measured through extended reach (to the right target audience) and repeated frequency (repeated over and over again.)

Some people in the publishing industry have referred to "editorial vs. advertising" as a "church vs. state separation."

This paid content is controlled by advertisers and generates the revenue to support the costs of the staff, the print, and the distribution.

The editors, on the other hand, write unbiased content for the reader.

COMPUTERS: A GAME CHANGER

Until websites became popular, traditional marketing (through advertising or editorial) was one of the few ways brands could control their message to ensure they reached their target audience.

I remember working on a black and white DOS computer in 1997. It was really exciting to think that were be able to connect with people and companies around the world just by the click of a mouse.

During this time, I was responsible for the design, architecture, and launch of our organization's website. It was approximately five pages with text and images that essentially acted as an online brochure. The purpose of this website was to provide online "brochure-ware" so that we could highlight what our organization did, some statistics about the benefits of our organization, and how you could get in touch with us. This marketing was really cutting-edge!

When Google began to gain popularity in 1998/1999, our capacity to search became much easier. (Thanks to Vincent Cerf, who is considered the "father of the Internet," and Sir Tim Berners-Lee who created the World Wide Web.)

From 1999-2000, I worked at a "dot-com" called Mediconsult. We worked with clients such as Eli Lilly (Prozac) and Novartis to help educate people looking for information about chronic conditions such as depression and hypertension. During this time, I worked on the marketing team as an "Interactive Marketing Specialist" to seed newsgroups and forums about the benefits of these drugs. At the time, this was an innovative way to connect in a two-way dialogue with the target audience for our pharmaceutical clients.

Many websites during the dot-com era were finding ways to disrupt the way we connected with each other. A social networking service called Six Degrees (1997-2001) allowed users to upload a profile and make friends with other users. Six Degrees was followed by other social networking sites including MySpace, Friendster, and LinkedIn.

In 2003, a Harvard University student named Mark Zuckerberg wrote a program called Facemash which was first launched for Harvard students only. In 2006 the whole world changed when Facebook allowed anyone over the age of 13 to have an account. By 2009, over 500 million[1] of us were members on Facebook and we were delighted to find a way to connect (and re-connect) with friends and family. As of 2016, Facebook has over 1.71 billion monthly active users.[2]

With the global adoption of Facebook, many of us now had a new method of communication that enabled us to connect person-to-person, business-to-person, and person-to-business at the click of a mouse.

This new form of communication allowed us to become "prosumers."[3] Coined by futurist Alvin Toffler and then re-introduced by author Don Tapscott, prosumers allow us to both produce and consume information.

Social media allowed mass communication to shift from one-to-many to one-to-one communication. The monologue has become a dialogue.

PERMISSION VS. PUSH

For businesses and brands (including you as a brand), the power of social media comes from its foundation in permission-based marketing.

This term was coined by author and entrepreneur Seth Godin in his book, *Permission Marketing: Turning Strangers into Friends and Friends into Customers.*[4]

Godin states that instead of annoying potential customers by interrupting them, marketing strategies should earn the privilege of delivering relevant messages to people who want to receive them.

A permission-based audience is likely to be much smaller than casting a wide net to a largely anonymous audience, but when your audience pre-qualifies themselves and raises their hand to say "Yes! I want to receive more information about your business," they are much more receptive to your messages.

(In Module #3, we will dive deeper into how you can use

permission-based marketing effectively for your brand.)

What excites me about the Social Media Revolution is how these channels have allowed brands to level the corporate playing field. Traditionally, only big brands could afford to connect with their target audience. Now we all have access to connect with the world on a massive scale.

As Tom Peters says in *The Brand Called You*[5]:
"You're not an 'employee' of General Motors, you're not a 'staffer' at General Mills, you're not a 'worker' at General Electric or a 'human resource' at General Dynamics (oops, it's gone!) Forget the Generals! You don't 'belong to' any company for life, and your chief affiliation isn't to any particular 'function.' You're not defined by your job title and you're not confined by your job description.
Starting today you are a brand."

MODULE #1 IS MADE UP OF THESE LESSONS:

Lesson #1: Who Are You?
Lesson #2: What is the ROI of You?
Lesson #3: You Are the MVP in Your UVP
Lesson #4: Facing Your Fear of Putting Yourself Out There.
Lesson #5: How to Handle a Public Relations Crisis.
Lesson #6: The Trail Of Your Digital Footprint.
Lesson #7: How Well Do You Know Your Ideal Client?
Lesson #8: What's Your Ideal Client Avatar's Story?
Lesson #9: Create Your Professional Presence Using LinkedIn.
Lesson #10: Get "Social Proof" Via Testimonials.
Lesson #11: Use Thought Leadership To Dominate Your
　　　　　　Niche.

LESSON #1

WHO ARE YOU?

Well, who are you?
(Who are you? Who, who, who, who?)
I really wanna know
(Who are you? Who, who, who, who?)
~The Who

In my business, I work with executives to craft and optimize their LinkedIn profiles. The one thing that has surprised me most is how often accomplished professionals admit to me how uncomfortable they feel having the spotlight shone on themselves.

Writing your bio can be challenging. It took me approximately six hours to write my own profile. It can take from five to ten hours to craft them for the executives I work with.

The reason this takes so much time is because we want to convey an interesting, relevant story about ourselves and our career that fascinates the reader. We also have to synthesize how amazing we are to within a 2,000-character count.

I love this quote by Blaise Pascal: *"I would have written a shorter letter, but I did not have the time.*[6]"

It takes a lot more time to pare down the copy so that it makes a strong first impression. One of the easiest ways to begin crafting your story is by defining who you are, what you do, and how you help your target audience.

Quite simply, what makes you different than everybody else?

What *empowers* you? What makes you tick? What makes you happy? Your core values help guide your behavior. They align with your beliefs. They affect your decisions and highlight what makes you unique.

People buy from you because of the *value* you bring to the relationship. People connect with you because they *get* you, and they trust you.

Why do you do what you do?

Globally recognized leadership expert, Simon Sinek says *"people don't buy what you do, they buy WHY you do it[7]."*

Some of your core values may include:

Accomplished	Clever	Direct	Expressive
Accountable	Collaborative	Disciplined	Extrovert
Accurate	Committed	Discreet	Fair
Adaptable	Compassionate	Diverse	Faithful
Adventurous	Confident	Dominant	Famous
Affectionate	Consistent	Down-to-earth	Fast
Agile	Cooperative	Dreamer	Fearless
Aggressive	Cordial	Driven	Ferocious
Ambitious	Courageous	Dutiful/Eager	Fierce
Appreciative	Courteous	Economic	Firm
Approachable	Crafty	Educated	Flexible
Assertive	Credible	Elegant	Fluent
Attentive	Curious	Empathetic	Focused
Balanced	Customer-fo-	Empowering	Formal
Bold	cused	Entertaining	Free-spirited
Brave	Daring	Enthusiastic	Fresh
Brilliant	Decisive	Equitable	Friendly
Calm	Dedicated	Ethical	Frugal
Capable	Dependable	Excellent	Fun
Careful	Determined	Exhilarated	Generous
Charitable	Devoted	Exuberant	Genius
Clear-minded	Diligent	Expert	Giving

Good	Mature	Qualified	Spirited
Grateful	Mellow	Quality	Spontaneous
Happy	Meticulous	Rational	Stealth
Hard-working	Mindful	Real	Strong
Harmonious	Moderate	Realistic	Structured
Helpful	Modest	Reasonable	Successful
Heroic	Mystery	Recognizable	Supportive
Historical	Neat	Refined	Sustainable
Honest	Obedient	Reflective	Sympathetic
Hopeful	Open-minded	Relation-	Synergistic
Hospitable	Optimistic	ship-driven	Systemized
Humble	Organized	Relaxed	Talented
Humorous	Original	Reliable	Teamwork
Hygienic	Outrageous	Resilient	Temperance
Imaginative	Passionate	Resolute	Thankful
Impactful	Patient	Resolved	Timely
Impartial	Patient-focused	Resourceful	Tolerant
Independent	Patriotic	Respectful	Tough
Informal	Peaceful	Responsive	Traditional
Innovative	People-focused	Restrained	Trained
Inquisitive	Perceptive	Results-oriented	Tranquil
Insightful	Perfectionist	Reverent	Transparent
Inspirational	Perseverance	Rigorous	Trustworthy
Integrity	Persuasive	Risk-taker	Understanding
Intelligent	Philanthropic	Sacrifice	Unflappable
Intense	Playful	Safety	Unique
Intuitive	Pleasant	Sanitary	Universal
Inventive	Poised	Secure	Useful
Inviting	Polished	Self-aware	Valor
Irreverent	Popular	Self-motivated	Value-driven
Joyful	Positive	Selfless	Variety
Judicial	Powerful	Sense of Humor	Victorious
Kind	Practical	Sensitive	Vigorous
Knowledgeable	Precise	Serene	Virtuous
Leader	Prepared	Serious	Visionary
Legal	Proud	Sharing	Warm
Level-headed	Private	Shrewd	Watchful
Liberal	Proactive	Significant	Wealthy
Lively	Professional	Silent	Welcoming
Logical	Profitable	Silly	Willful
Loveable	Prosperous	Simple	Winning
Lovely	Prudent	Sincere	Wise
Loyal	Punctual	Skillful	
Master	Pure	Smart	

EXERCISE #1: DEFINE YOUR CORE VALUES AND YOUR "WHY"

TIME COMMITMENT: 15 MINUTES

One of the easiest ways to begin the process of telling your story is by defining your *why*. Write down at least three core values that define who you are:

1. _____
_____
_____
_____
_____
_____

2. _____
_____
_____
_____
_____
_____

3. _____
_____
_____
_____

Note: According to Entrepreneur.com[8], do not use any of the following overused buzzwords on your LinkedIn profile:

Creative	Track record
Organizational	Innovative
Effective	Responsible
Motivated	Analytical
Extensive experience	Problem-solving

Now, write a short paragraph about WHY you do what you do:

_____
_____
_____
_____
_____
_____
_____
_____
_____
_____
_____
_____
_____
_____
_____
_____
_____
_____
_____
_____
_____
_____
_____
_____
_____
_____
_____
_____
_____
_____

LESSON #2

WHAT IS THE ROI
OF YOU?

"I'm looking for a dare to be great situation."

~Say Anything

"What's the ROI?"

I'm asked this question all the time. ROI stands for "Return on Investment."

Defined by Investopedia.com, ROI is:

"A performance measure used to evaluate the efficiency of an investment or to compare the efficiency of a number of different investments. ROI measures the amount of return on an investment relative to the investment's cost.

To calculate ROI, the benefit (or return) of an investment is divided by the cost of the investment, and the result is expressed as a percentage or a ratio.[9]"

ROI is usually defined by monetary investment, but have you ever thought about the ROI of YOU?

What is the benefit for your clients in investing in you, divided by the cost?

Some of these benefits can be intrinsic or extrinsic.

Extrinsic benefits may include how you help them or the physical and tangible value that you provide. Intrinsic benefits are often intangible, and are usually described by the feelings you elicit.

EXTRINSIC BENEFITS	INTRINSIC BENEFITS
• Make more money • Save money • Generate awareness	• Feeling of pleasure • Confidence • Trust

To find the ROI, your intrinsic and/or extrinsic benefits are divided by the cost of trust, financial investment, fear of failure and/or embarrassment.

SETTING YOUR GOALS AND MEASURING YOUR METRICS

"Would you tell me, please, which way I ought to go from here?"

"That depends a good deal on where you want to get to," said the Cat.

"I don't much care where," said Alice.

"Then it doesn't matter which way you go," said the Cat.

"So long as I get SOMEWHERE," Alice added as an explanation.

"Oh, you're sure to do that," said the Cat, "if you only walk long enough."

—Lewis Carroll, Alice in Wonderland

I often think of this quote when clients or people tell me "everyone" is their target audience. I get it, defining an audience can be tough. You're afraid that you're going to exclude everybody else, right? Here's the catch: once you've defined a niche, people are more likely to gravitate towards you. Like the Cheshire Cat implies, "any path" will take you to a random destination if you don't have a plan and a strategy in place.

In any business/brand, the mission, vision, and goals drive the big idea to outline:

- What you want to achieve (mission)?
- How you will achieve your mission (vision)?
- The key performance indicators (KPIs) about what you need to do to meet your objectives (goals)?

It's crucial that you set a clear process about what you want, the resources you need to do to get there, and how long it will take.

Some of the goals are measurable (quantitative), and some of them aren't (qualitative).

Take a few moments to think about why you want to create a brand for yourself.

Do you want to:

- Be the industry thought leader and expert?
- Generate new high-quality leads?
- Build brand awareness for yourself and/or your company?
- Improve the perception of your brand in the marketplace?
- Keep your current clients happy and loyal?
- Obtain more referrals?
- Be invited for guest appearances on tv, radio, blogs, podcasts, etc.
- Win honors or awards.
- Get more traffic to your website or blog.
- Develop an online community (or tribe) within your niche.
- Accomplish another goal not listed here?

MEASURE WHAT MATTERS

In the early days of social media, the number of followers on social media was a key performance indicator (KPI) that many brands used to determine success.

While the number of followers can be a good thing, this KPI is a kind of "vanity" metric. People can have thousands of followers, but how many people actually see and engage with your posts?

For example, when I hit the 5,000 follower mark on Twitter, I was really pleased and proud to have achieved this milestone. It wasn't a huge number for well-recognized brands, but for an entrepreneur, I thought this was a good metric. When I looked at the number of people who actually saw or engaged with my posts, I could see that the number of my followers who were actually consuming my content was significantly less than 5,000 people.

It's much more important to measure engagement, reach, leads and conversions than it is to measure the total number of followers because followers can be purchased. Engagement is a much more effective indicator of success because it is earned and generates valuable word-of-mouth awareness.

EXERCISE #2: SET SMART GOALS FOR DEVELOPING YOUR BRAND

TIME COMMITMENT: 20 MINUTES

To be successful, you want to set S.M.A.R.T goals. This acronym stands for Specific, Measurable, Attainable, Realistic, and Time Bound.

For each goal, write down what you want, the resources you need to get what you want, and when you expect to have the goal accomplished. Then, in your calendar, assign specific times you will work on these goals, and set milestones for certain accomplishments.

Specific Goal	What do you want to accomplish? Why is it important to you?	
Measurable	How will you measure success?	
Achievable	Is this goal reasonable? What are the steps you need to take? Who can help you achieve this goal?	
Realistic/ Relevant	When is the right time to accomplish this goal? Do you have all the resources you need?	
Time-Bound	Is it a short-term or long-term goal? How long will it take to complete your goal? When will you work on it? Set a reasonable "work back" schedule to ensure you stay on track.	

BONUS POINTS:

Do you have one big, giant, over-the-top goal? Be sure to write it down, too. Shoot for the stars!

IMAGINE THIS

Having just set some goals for yourself, I want to you "play" with me here. Imagine yourself at a time in the near future when you have completed all the exercises in this book, and have launched *you* as a brand. (This may sound "woo-woo", but stay with me here, it will work. You want to be a superstar brand, right?)

Take a moment to get centered. Now, close your eyes and picture what you look like and how you'll sound when you've accomplished your biggest goal as a polished, professional brand. When you've achieved your goal, what will you feel like? Think about all your senses, and breathe in your abundance.

While you imagine yourself in the future, smile as you reflect upon how far you've come and how it feels to be a successful, well-recognized brand which is adored by many people.

Remember to *really* embody your future self: feel what you feel, see what you see, and hear what you hear, by being a successful brand.

Do this exercise for a few minutes with your eyes closed and your imagination set on your future self. When you're ready to come back to the exercises, take and deep breath, smile, and get ready for more fun.

Take a few minutes and do this *right* now. (I'll wait.)

LESSON #3

YOU ARE THE MVP IN YOUR UVP

"Strange, isn't it? Each man's life touches so many other lives. When he isn't around he leaves an awful hole, doesn't he?"

~It's a Wonderful Life

Your UVP (Unique Value Proposition), can also be called your POD (Point of Differentiation). It includes a "promise" of what you do with specific benefits. It outlines who you are, how you help your specific target audience, and highlights why you're different than everyone else.

What do you want to be known for? Or, how do you want people to remember you? What are the specific benefits that only you can deliver?

WHAT KIND OF BRAND DO YOU WANT TO BE?

Think of some of the most popular business brands:

Coca-Cola	Google	Microsoft	Toyota	Samsung
Apple	McDonald's	Amazon	BMW	Disney
Nike	Louis Vuitton	L'Oreal	Tiffany	Porsche

Now think about some of the most famous people (alive or dead):

Marilyn Monroe	Elvis Presley	Oprah Winfrey	Michael Jackson
Tom Cruise	Albert Einstein	Katy Perry	Madonna
Cristiano Ronaldo	Mother Teresa	Nelson Mandela	Mohammad Ali

- Can you describe each brand with one word?
- What appeals to you about this brand?
- What makes them unique?

With your favourite brand(s), can you apply the same principles to your professional brand?

BUILD YOUR STORY WITH THE "KNOW, LIKE, AND TRUST" FACTOR

Sales and persuasion are built on a foundation of trust. Some people even refer to the "know, like, and trust" factor as the primary reason your target audience buys from you.

You build trust through each gesture or micro-moment at a time. You prove your trust through consistency and commitment and by providing value first. (We will go a lot deeper into these concepts in Lesson #15)

I absolutely *love* this quote about value and trust from Michael Port's book, *Book Yourself Solid*. He says:

> *"Your ideal clients - so long as they need what you're selling - will make investments that are directly proportional to the amount of trust that they have in you."*[10]

Port also says:

> *"There are only two ways to build trust: Do what you say you're going to do, and deliver what you say you're going to deliver."*

Think about this for a moment. Products you buy at the Dollar Store don't require much trust because these products are very small investments. But if your prospect is investing a lot of time or money, then you have to build a lot of trusts before they open up their wallets.

A smart strategy to build trust is through incremental commitments. Provide free offers or content first, then level up to a small investment, and continue to build trust while increasing the price point.

HIT 'EM IN "THE FEELS"

We almost always buy because of an emotional reason: we just feel it in our gut.

We then substantiate and justify why we buy with logic and statistics.

We use our instincts to guide us to trust the process. We also make purchase decisions because of the way it makes us *feel*.

As Dr. Maya Angelou said:

> *"...people will forget what you said, people will forget what you did, but people never forget how you made them feel*[11]*."*

For a moment, think about how your audience sees you and how they feel about you from their perspective.

WHY DOES THE ROI OF YOU MATTER?

Every single one of us who are using digital platforms and social media are now media agencies. You have the opportunity to connect, personalize, and deepen relationships using tools such as LinkedIn, Facebook, Twitter, blogging and more.

You probably already know that Justin Bieber was "discovered" thanks to a video on YouTube. Other famous YouTubers have become their own multi-million brands including "Smosh," "PewtiePie," Miranda Sings, Hannah Hart from "My Drunk Kitchen," Bethany Mota, or Jenna Marbles.

You may not have heard of these people, but ask any ten-year-old and they will tell you who these people are.

I was shocked to see that some of the famous Minecraft YouTube gamers have even launched a line of action figures and plushies. Now *that* is building a brand!

How did these people start? By putting themselves "out there," one video and one piece of content at a time.

As a part of your overall brand, the content is a key part, but you also want to think about:

- your look (including colors you use, if you have your logo, the typeface, the way you dress etc.).
- the feel of your brand (your tone of written or verbal language, the way you express yourself through interactions, etc.).
- your reputation (what others say about you).

I was once told that my bubbly personality didn't come across as well on my old website at www.punchmedia.ca. I took some steps to include videos and tailored the language on my site to make it align better with my personality.

How important is your overall brand? According to LinkedIn, 81% of buyers report that they're likely to engage with sellers who have a strong, professional brand.[13]

In social media, and through Google Search Engine Optimization, LinkedIn is one of the highest ranked sites when someone Googles your name[12]. It's imperative that you create a really strong first impression that fascinates and "wows" the reader.

You, too, can dominate as a thought leader within your niche by publishing relevant, quality content that resonates with your target audience.

Let's get started with what makes you different than everyone else.

EXERCISE #3: CONSTRUCT YOUR UNIQUE VALUE PROPOSITION

TIME COMMITMENT: 20 MINUTES

Your unique value proposition highlights what you do, your target audience, and how you deliver results.

A great video to watch and inspire you before building your unique value proposition is Simon Sinek's TED Talk called *How Great Leaders Inspire Action.*

Fill-in-the-blanks:

I'm _____ about helping _____
   (emotion)   (target audience)

to _____ by _____
        (results you deliver)   (how you do what you do)

because _____.
                   (your why)

Now, write out this information as one paragraph "story" that defines why you do what you do, who you help, and how you help them.

For example:

Financial Advisor

I'm passionate about helping people grow and optimize their financial net worth by doing a thorough audit of your current financial situation, setting specific goals, and continuously measuring and monitoring results so that I ensure your financial investments stay on track.

Insurance Agent

I believe family comes first. My father was an insurance agent, and I became involved in this industry because I saw how he helped protect families from financial disasters.

Leadership Role (C-Suite) or Human Resources

I love helping grow strong, successful teams of people so that our company can maximize value and increase our competitive advantage. I do so by inspiring and motivating our team members and allowing them to step into their power through problem-solving and providing mentorship.

Now that you can highlight your value proposition, when people ask you what you do, you can tell them in 30 seconds or less!

Now it's your turn.

_____

_____

_____

_____

_____

_____

_____

_____

_____

_____

_____

_____

_____

_____

_____

_____

_____

_____

_____

_____

_____

LESSON #4

FACING YOUR FEAR OF PUTTING YOURSELF "OUT THERE"

"People call those imperfections, but no, that's the good stuff."

~Good Will Hunting

Have you ever felt like you weren't enough? Have you ever thought "why the heck would people ever listen to me?"

The perception you have about yourself can often be completely different than the perception others have about you.

I've had strangers come up to me after a presentation and say "How do you do it all?" And I turn around to see if they are talking to the person behind me.

One time after speaking at a very well-attended conference, I read through the feedback and comments from the attendees.

Ninety-nine percent of the responses were positive and reassuring. They said lovely things such as:

"The speaker provided a lot of great information I could implement right away."

"She has a lot of enthusiasm. I really enjoyed this presentation."

As I pored through all the responses, quickly gliding past all the positive comments, I noticed that I was actively looking for the negative feedback so that I could validate to myself that I wasn't enough.

There it was.

One person responded with:

"She seemed a little manic."

At that very moment, I realized I was eagerly looking for the negative feedback instead of enjoying the praise. Yes. I *do* sometimes come across as a little manic. I talk too fast because I am very energetic when I speak. (I really love what I do.) Even though I do my very best to make sure each and every presentation is filled with enthusiasm, entertainment, and actionable takeaways, I now know that everyone isn't going to like me.

Perhaps I remind them of someone they don't like.

Perhaps the reason they don't like me has nothing to do with me at all.

Perhaps their energy is on a different level than mine, and they would connect better with someone who is much more sedate than I am.

And that's *okay*.

In this world of abundance, there is a perfect speaker that is just right for them.

THE POWER OF VULNERABILITY

I absolutely adore Dr. Brené Brown's TED Talk where she discusses *The Power of Vulnerability*.[14]

What I've learned from Dr. Brown's work is that we tend to admire people who put themselves "out there." We think people who show their vulnerability are very brave. But, when we personally become vulnerable, we consider it a weakness in our character. We want to hide our vulnerability for fear of being exposed.

"...True belonging only happens when we present our authentic, imperfect selves to the world. Our sense of belonging can never be greater than our level of self-acceptance."

— Dr. Brené Brown

FINDING THE PERFECT IN IMPERFECTION

I recently came across a Japanese concept that brought a giant smile to my face. The term is called "wabi-sabi" and is defined as:

> "a world view or aesthetic centered on the acceptance of transience and imperfection. The aesthetic is sometimes described as one of beauty that is imperfect, impermanent, and incomplete."
>
> —Leonard Koren,
> author of *Wabi-Sabi: for Artists, Designers, Poets & Philosophers*[15]

What a beautiful concept! The beauty is in the imperfection. The things you may think are flaws may be some of the most endearing parts of your personality.

It's your belief of imperfection that can hold you back from launching. Why? Because we want everything to be perfect so people will be less likely to reject us.

Doing nothing is easy. Taking the steps to move forward can be challenging, but it can also the most rewarding. Instead of fearing failure, we have to remind ourselves that it's time to embrace the possibility of what we could be if we embrace our "wabi-sabi" and soar!

Striving for true perfection isn't feasible. No one is perfect. Besides, being perfect would be downright *boring*!

RE-DEFINING FAILURE

"You build on failure. You use it as a stepping stone. Close the door on the past. You don't try to forget the mistakes, but you don't dwell on it. You don't let it have any of your energy, or any of your time, or any of your space." [16]

—Johnny Cash

There are hundreds (maybe even thousands) of quotes about failure. Many coaches and organizations who encourage innovation will tell you to "fail fast, and fail often."

To keep moving forward, you have to get comfortable feeling uncomfortable.

There are two very important reasons we hold ourselves back:

- Most of us were always raised to put others before ourselves (in my opinion, this particularly is true if you're a female).
- Our brain is naturally designed to trigger fear so that it protects us and keep us from getting hurt.

Without getting too scientific, our brain has an area called the limbic cortex called the amygdala which is the area responsible for fear, as well as other emotions. As animals, fear and instincts are designed to protect us instinctively from predators. We universally fear rejection and seek approval. To override your fears, you can reframe them, and find ways to do it anyway.

Just remember: you're not alone. Even the most successful people feel the exact same way. Barbra Streisand, Andrea Bocelli, and Adele have all publicly stated they have stage fright.

FILL YOUR BUCKET

At my son's school, the teachers and the students were discussing a concept from the book *Have You Filled A Bucket Today?*, by Carol McCloud which asks: "are you a bucket filler or a bucket dipper?"

A bucket filler is someone who shows kindness and love towards others. A bucket dipper is someone who is unkind and makes fun of someone or ignores them.

I adored that my son's school was addressing ways to encourage positive behavior and "pay it forward."

A few months later, I realized this concept could be taken a bit further by attending my own high school reunion.

I was having a conversation with Darren Vance at our reunion about some of the fun times we had at our school. Darren was the real-life version of Jake Ryan from the movie *Sixteen Candles*. He was captain of the football team, he was elected by his peers to be a representative on the Student Council, and was also a super friendly guy to everyone in the school regardless of the grade they were in.

I mentioned to Darren at the reunion that he was "the guy every girl wanted to date and whom every boy wanted to be like." His reply surprised the heck out of me. He immediately confessed how much he *hated* high school because he felt really insecure during those years.

Wait! Whaaat? (Insert scratching record sound here.)

This is a guy who appeared to have it all together. He seemed confident. He dated all the pretty girls. He was popular and accomplished, and he was a really nice guy on top of it all.

It goes to show you, no matter how things may appear on the outside, there is a big difference between the perception of how we feel about ourselves versus the way we appear to others. I realized that the bucket-filling concept has a great foundation, but we also have to be responsible for filling our *own* bucket first.

This way, you don't need to rely on other people to fill up your bucket, and your bucket will be far too heavy for the "dippers" to tip over. Because there will always be dippers, critics and naysayers who will try.

"IT'S NOT THE CRITIC WHO COUNTS"

The concept of reframing fear was one of the most powerful lessons I learned when I took my NLP Practitioner course with Elizabeth Payea-Butler.

NLP teaches us that to reframe, you can simply look at the situation from another perspective.

During Dr. Brené Brown's TED Talk, she shared the following quote from Theodore Roosevelt. This quote still gives me goosebumps, as it has helped me take the "power" away from some people who criticize:

> "It is not the critic who counts; not the man who points out how the strong man stumbles, or where the doer of deeds could have done them better. The credit belongs to the man who is actually in the arena, whose face is marred by dust and sweat and blood; who strives valiantly; who errs, who comes short again and again, because there is no effort without error and shortcoming; but who does actually strive to do the deeds; who knows great enthusiasms, the great devotions; who spends himself in a worthy cause; who at the best knows in the end the triumph of high achievement, and who at the worst, if he fails, at least fails while daring greatly, so that his place shall never be with those cold and timid souls who neither know victory nor defeat.[17]"

What this quote means to me is that if people criticize, but they aren't *in* the arena, with blood, sweat, and tears, doing what I do, then it's easy for them to lean back with their arms folded (and a scowl on their face) while saying "I wouldn't have done it that way."

Sometimes these people are known as "armchair critics". They have no experience doing what you do, but they have all sorts of advice about how they would do it differently.

They may have the best intentions by providing their feedback. They may believe that their feedback will help, but if they haven't been in your shoes, doing what you're doing, it's *easy* for them to say how they would have done it differently.

So instead of worrying about or being afraid of what the critics say, remember that *you* are the one who is "walking the walk" instead of just "talking the talk."

And if that quote doesn't help, think about the darling Del Griffith (played by John Candy) from the movie *Planes, Trains & Automobiles*, when he says to the uptight Neal Page (played by Steve Martin):

> "You wanna hurt me? Go right ahead if it makes you feel any better. I'm an easy target. Yeah, you're right, I talk too much. I also listen too much. I could be a cold-hearted cynic like you....but I don't like to hurt people's feelings. Well, you think what you want about me; I'm not changing. I like....I like me. My wife likes me. My customers like me. 'Cause I'm the real article. What you see is what you get."

I'd much rather be a Del Griffith than a Neal Page, wouldn't you? Everyone has fears, but they don't have to prevent you from taking action. Even a small "baby step" forward can get you moving in the right direction. Forget about perfection; no one is perfect. Let go of whatever limiting beliefs you have about yourself. Imagine how great you'll feel to shift your self-doubt into empowerment!

EXERCISE #4: WRITE DOWN AT LEAST ONE WAY YOU CAN REFRAME NEGATIVE THOUGHTS OR COMMENTS.

TIME COMMITMENT: 5 MINUTES

Write down at least one way you can reframe negative thoughts or comments. You may wish to include you own quotes or perspective about how to take the power away from the critics and set reminders to let yourself shine.

_____
_____
_____
_____
_____
_____
_____
_____
_____
_____
_____
_____
_____
_____
_____
_____
_____
_____
_____
_____
_____
_____
_____

LESSON #5:

HOW TO HANDLE A PUBLIC RELATIONS CRISIS.

"Did you know that 'if' is the middle word in life?"

~Apocalypse Now

Someone once said to me: *"The best thing about social media is that everyone has a voice. The worst thing about social media is that everyone has a voice."*

When it comes to social media, a common fear my clients have shared with me has been: *"what will happen if someone says something bad about my business?"*

My response has always been the following:

When you do good work, people won't publish negative information about you.

If someone publishes a negative comment, it can often be a great learning opportunity for your business. Social media allows you to listen to the conversation so that you can address them and make amends. This way, other prospects can see you are doing your very best to ensure you're giving great service. (One way to mitigate an argument is to ask the person to provide you with their phone number or email address so you can take the conversation offline.)

And quite simply, "haters gonna hate."

Pro Tip: Never argue with trolls, because their whole mission is to stir up conflict with negative posts.

Despite the point above, I had to face my own Public Relations crisis in 2010. A mutual acquaintance forwarded an email from Ann* which read:

"If you've been happy with the work I've done for you, I'd appreciate you adding your two cents to counteract a smear campaign my competitor has just launched on my blog..."

Within the email was a link to a blog post that read:

Leslie Hughes Says:
September 21st, 2010 at 8:42 am

You are a hack Ann*and we both know it, you have stepped on a lot of toes and people talk in this town.

Stop trying to peddle your webinars, you don't know how to use social media properly yourself and they make you look like the money grubbing pig that you are.

*Names have been changed for anonymity

I was horrified to read these horrible words written alongside my name, my email, and my photo.

Within eight hours, 40 people had responded to say things such as *"Leslie, you're a horrible person,"* and *"Would you kiss your mother with that mouth?"*

My initial reaction was deep empathy for Ann* who had thought I *had* written these words. Secondly, I thought this lie, written on a public blog, was going to annihilate the new business I had just launched.

Lastly, and most importantly, I immediately became hyper aware of the digital footprint I had created for myself, and for my child, who was only three-years-old at that time.

I had a lot of awful emotions swirling inside me during that time: anger, fear, frustration, and a deep feeling of vulnerability. As a proud mom, I had uploaded several photos of my son and our family dog, Harley. I probably had unknowingly shared where my son went to pre-school and published a pattern of where we lived and what we were doing. I worried that I had shared information that could make my child vulnerable to being kidnapped.

I asked myself, "if this person was intent on damaging my professional reputation, what could they do to my personal life?"

Could this person have gone to my son's school, approached my child, and said: "Hi Brady! Your mom has been in a terrible accident, and she asked me to come and get you from school. I have Harley in the car. C'mon, let's go"?

This one post had changed the way I used social media...forever!

I also realized that my child was much too young to give me permission to share his image online, and I wondered if there would be a time in the future when my son would say to me, "Mom, I don't like that you've shared all these photos of me online. I wish you had never done this."

I'm sure you can imagine that this was a very difficult and challenging time for me.

Why would anyone want to harm my reputation and potentially ruin my career? And who could have done this?

I discussed this situation with my lifelong friend, who is a Staff Sergeant. He suggested I go to my local police department with my documentation and quote the Canadian Criminal Code 403C, which covers identity fraud:

IDENTITY FRAUD

403 (1) Everyone commits an offence who fraudulently personates
another person, living or dead,

(a) with intent to gain advantage for themselves or another person;

(b) with intent to obtain any property or an interest in any property;

(c) with intent to cause disadvantage to the person being personated or
another person; or

(d) with intent to avoid arrest or prosecution or to obstruct, pervert or
defeat the course of justice.

Marginal note: Clarification (2) For the purposes of subsection (1),
personating a person includes pretending to be the person or using the
person's identity information — whether by itself or in combination with
identity information pertaining to any person — as if it pertains to the
person using it.

Marginal note: Punishment (3) Everyone who commits an offence
under subsection (1)

(a) is guilty of an indictable offence and liable to imprisonment for a
term of not more than 10 years; or

(b) is guilty of an offence punishable on summary conviction[18].

(Remember, this was *way* back in 2010 when the laws hadn't caught
up with the Internet just yet.)

I spoke with Ann* on the phone, and she provided me with the
IP address of the person who wrote the post on her blog. I went to
my local police station with the IP address, a printed copy of the 40
comments that said I was a horrible business person, and my three-
year-old toddler in tow.

Thankfully, D/C Pallister at the Durham Regional Police Department
documented all my information, obtained a search warrant, and found
out the IP address belonged to an 80-something-year-old woman who
was living with her 40-something-year-old son (let's call him Dan.)

Dan admitted to D/C Pallister that he used my name on Ann's* blog
and used my name on this horrible post "for fun." He said he didn't
have anything against me personally, but was too afraid to use his own
name when he wrote those awful things to Ann* online.

As a part of his penance, Dan was required to do community service. (He also had to write me a testimonial, but I don't think I'm ever going to use this in my marketing material.)

Yes, Dan admitted he had turned my life upside down...for *fun*?!?

I never met Dan in person. He had been following me via social media, and we had even exchanged a few tweets, but we never met in real life. I never thought a virtual stranger would ever want to cause my family or me any harm.

The ultimate irony was this: I teach people how to use social media properly and optimize their privacy, only to have my *own* online identity violated.

Was there anything I could have done prevent this from happening to me? No.

Social media is an open forum. People impersonate others by creating fictitious accounts (sometimes called "catfishing") all the time. This can happen to anyone, whether or not they are actively using social media.

I was relieved that this situation was resolved within a month, but what was I going to do about my professional reputation?

I couldn't have prevented this situation from happening to me, but I could control how I handled the situation. It was my first lesson in Public Relations 101.

My friend and mentor Anita Windisman suggested I write a blog on my own website to tell my side of the story. Anita suggested I use this as an opportunity to frame the story as if I was advising my clients in case this ever happened to them.

HOW TO HANDLE A PUBLIC RELATIONS CRISIS

Step #1: If possible, be ready in advance with a plan to handle a "worst-case scenario".

Can you determine possible risks ahead of time? Practice and refine your crisis management plan regularly to ensure everyone is up-to-date and ready to take action.

Step #2: Notify your target audience with a blog post (if you are a sole proprietor). Observe the proper chain of command right away. You'll want to ensure senior management is aware of the situation (if you work for a larger organization).

Be as "human" as possible. People prefer to connect with people. No one likes a canned, corporate response.

Step #3: Update your audience and respond to the incident as soon as possible. Social media moves *fast*. The earlier you address the crisis, the less likely it will go "viral".

Let your audience know the progress of the situation if possible.

If a mistake has been made, apologize sincerely and acknowledge how you will be taking the appropriate steps to rectify the situation.

Engage with your target audience by responding to their questions and concerns.

Thankfully, this situation didn't permanently hurt the image of my brand, but I now share this story to let people know that if it can happen to me, it can happen to anyone.

I'm obviously still very passionate about all of the benefits of social media. I'm just also very aware of the types of content I publish, and the digital footprint we leave behind.

EXERCISE #5: PLAN FOR YOUR WORST CASE SCENARIO

TIME COMMITMENT: 10 MINUTES

What is the worst thing that could happen to your brand and reputation? How would you handle it?

_____

_____

_____

_____

_____

_____

_____

_____

_____

_____

_____

_____

_____

_____

_____

_____

_____

_____

_____

_____

_____

_____

_____

_____

_____

_____

LESSON #6

THE TRAIL OF YOUR DIGITAL FOOTPRINT

"Parents can only give good advice or put them on the right paths, but the final forming of a person's character lies in their own hands."

~Anne Frank

Your digital footprint includes every piece of data that is captured or shared on websites or social media. This information (for the most part) is permanent. What goes on the Internet, stays on the Internet. Your digital footprint will be accessible for future generations to come. ("Hey guys...check out my great, great, great grandma with the duck-face selfie!")

Have *you* ever researched yourself through the eyes of your prospect or client?

As part of my curriculum, my students are required to complete a thorough audit of their online presence from the perspective of a recruiter or hiring manager. They have to Google their name, look at various sites, and answer the question: *"Would a company hire you based on your current presence on social media?"*

As a brand, your target audience will experience you from multiple touchpoints (which we will discuss in Lesson #15). A touchpoint is any time a potential client comes in contact with your brand.

Your brand isn't just what you say about yourself. As the founder of Amazon Jeff Bezos says:

"Your brand is what people say about you when you leave the room."

When was the last time you Googled your name? What did you find?

You probably have never taken the time to do this while pretending to be your ideal client or ideal target audience, have you?

This exercise is so very important because your marketing depends on how your target market sees you. You can better tailor your messages and dominate your niche once you *really* get to know who they are and what they want to know about.

To get in the mind of your ideal client, you're going to want to do your research.

This may sound creepy and "stalkerish" but the goal here is to *really* know the people you want to serve so you can deliver the content that they need.

From the perspective of your prospective client, think about:

- What is their first impression of you?
- What have they seen based on your online presence?
- What have they seen based on your in-person meeting?
- What are they saying to themselves?
- How do they feel?

To gain resonance and build trust with your target audience, you have to become a bit of a mind-reader. You have to let them know (often times before they even know they have a problem), that *you* are the perfect solution.

EXERCISE #6: AUDIT YOUR FIRST IMPRESSION

TIME COMMITMENT: 30+ MINUTES

Google your name. What sites appeared on the first page? What is the first impression you see of yourself? Does it effectively tell your story? What kinds of strategies can you use to improve your first impression?

We will do a deeper dive on this and how you can deepen these touchpoints on in Lesson #15, but let's get started with an initial first impression.

_____
_____
_____
_____
_____
_____
_____
_____
_____
_____
_____
_____
_____
_____
_____
_____
_____
_____
_____
_____
_____
_____

LESSON #7

DO YOU KNOW YOUR IDEAL CLIENT?

"You never really understand a person until you consider things from his point of view. Until you climb inside of his skin and walk around in it."

~To Kill a Mockingbird

The more you know your ideal client, the more effective your marketing will become. You will also be much more likely to attract the *right* clients who are the perfect fit for you.

Remember—"everyone" is not a strategy.

An ideal client avatar (ICA) is a fictional persona that represents your perfect client. This exercise is probably one of the most time-consuming, but also one of the most important things you can do to help you create your brand because it will help you to frame your messaging so that you reach the right people, using the right channels, at the right time.

Essentially you are "making it up." You are putting together the most common results by completing the worksheet below.

Top Tips:

- Look at the clients/target audience who produce the most profit for your business or who receive the best results from your work.
- Go to LinkedIn and search at least five people who have the same title as those in your target audience.
- Don't just stop at LinkedIn! Check out other social media channels to look at what they publish, and find out how your audience is engaging.
- Do your best to gather as much demographic and psychographic information you can gather. Demographic information specifies gender, age group, income levels, etc.; psychographics describes attitudes, values, or lifestyles.
- You may presume you know everything there is to know, but you might be surprised to find *new* information that can help you with your brand.

Understand what *really* drives them to do what they do. Remember to get in the mindset of your audience so that you can address all of their fears and frustrations.

Note: For each target audience segment you have, you will have to craft a separate and unique ideal client avatar. This is important because each target audience will have a unique set of values, principles, and perspectives. Your marketing and your messaging will change with each audience segment. If you do not tailor your messages properly, the content may not resonate, so be sure you complete each step.

EXERCISE #7: CREATE YOUR IDEAL CLIENT AVATAR BLUEPRINT

TIME COMMITMENT: 90+ MINUTES

Complete the following areas and include as many details as possible. This exercise is for your reference only, so be sure to use your imagination and have fun!

- Age
- Income
- Gender
- Marital Status
- Occupation
- How long has he/she worked there?
- Do they have employees? How many?
- How many people does he/she have to speak with during the decision-making process?
- What kind of car do they drive?
- What do they do in their spare time?
- Favorite books, TV shows, magazines
- Where do they turn to for breaking news?
- Social media channels they follow?
- Conferences and events they attend?
- What are their business goals?
- What are their personal/family goals?

Write down your target audience's top 5 pain points. What are their specific needs? (Or, if you're selling a luxury product, what are they buying into?)

_____

_____

_____

_____

_____

If they aren't the key decision maker, how will their boss react if they purchase your product/services?

_____

_____

_____

What are the 3 biggest objections about why they *won't* buy your products or services?

_____

_____

_____

What are they secretly afraid of? What are they too afraid to say out loud?

_____

_____

_____

What is the biggest result you provide, and how does it fit into their world from their perspective?

_____

_____

_____

What key emotions does your ideal client feel at the *exact* moment they are ready to buy your product/service or adopt your idea?

_____

_____

_____

If your ideal client had a magic wand and could have the perfect solution to their biggest problem, what would that perfect product/ service look like?

_____

_____

_____

_____

_____

_____

WHY WE BUY

I often say that marketing is "benevolent manipulation". Our goal as marketers is to build enough "yesses" along the sales funnel and gently persuade our target audience to buy our products or services (or "buy into" our ideas).

You have to be the right fit, at the right time, providing the right solution.

We rarely—if ever—buy anything of value on first glance.

There is a general "rule of thumb" that it takes between 8 to 12 brand impressions before you build brand resonance with your target audience.

Forrester Research[19] has specifically quantified the number as 11.4 touchpoints. This is how many pieces of content your target audience will connect with before they purchase. Google calls this moment of purchase "The Zero Moment of Truth" or "ZMOT[20]".

In today's information-based society, we are producing more than 2.5 quintillion bytes of data[21] each day. We can access just about anything online. The path to purchase has changed. Clients and consumers now have the power and opportunity to be as educated as the salesperson.

Your target audience is empowered with access to information, and is also more critical than ever before.

Remember how we discussed your amygdala and how it holds you back from your true potential? Well, those same fears can also hold your clients back from taking action and making decisions to purchase your products/services.

Some of your client's objections and fears may include:

- Complacency: *"That's not the way we did it in the past"* or *"I'm okay with my current provider."*
- Price: *"I can get the same results cheaper from someone else."*
- Personal politics: *"I have to go with my brother-in-law because he's family."*
- Trust: *"I don't know you well enough or believe you have the experience to be able to solve my problems."*

We will do a deeper dive to discuss these objections (and some ways to get around them) in Lesson #21. I want you to begin thinking about how you can make your prospective clients and current clients feel important and valued.

In your sales process, you'll build trust with your audience when you address some of these objections and follow up with the specific solutions you provide.

Be sure to research:

- The industry-specific words or acronyms (NGO, CPG, KPI, etc.) your target audience uses.
- The brands, companies, and influencers they follow on LinkedIn and Twitter.
- The various online groups have they have joined on LinkedIn.
- If they have completed a specific level of education, what field(s)?
- What kinds of connections do they have on LinkedIn?
- What they have recently posted on LinkedIn or other channels?
- If there is an online posting of their job requirements and/or a description of what they do in their current role.

LESSON #8

WHAT'S YOUR IDEAL CLIENT AVATAR'S STORY?

"What's the story, morning glory? What's the tale, nightingale?"

~Bye Bye Birdie

Your next step is to take the information you've learned about your ideal client avatar and actually craft a "story" that highlights who they are, along with some of the decision-making process they have to go through.

You'll go through their emotions, their fears, their problem(s), and steps they may take to find a solution.

Mapping out their journey can certainly help you be one step ahead of them, and can reassure them that you know how they are feeling, and you're there to help them with the perfect solution.

For example:

Client: James Smith

Fictional Role: Financial Advisor

James Smith is a 40 year-old, married, father of two daughters. He has just landed the new role of Vice President of Sales and Marketing for a well-known hotel company. His office is in downtown Toronto, and he makes $120,000 per year. James drives a silver BMW and lives in a suburb approximately 30 kilometers from his office. On summer weekends, he and his family drive up to their chalet in Collingwood. In the summer, their family hikes, mountain-bikes, and swims. In the winter, they ski at a local ski club. James loves the Toronto Blue Jays and attends several games each season with his kids or his friends.

James is responsible for overseeing a team of 15 senior managers across Canada. He and his team are expected to build and sustain revenue for the organization by driving the corporate message across traditional and digital channels, overseeing customer relationship management and new business development.

James subscribes to Marketing Magazine, Inc., Success, and Forbes. In his spare time, he reads books by John Grisham and business books by Seth Godin and Jeffrey Gitomer. He attends "The Art of Marketing" and "The Art of Sales" conferences in Toronto, and occasionally attends events at the Toronto Board of Trade.

Challenge: James already has a financial advisor who he's been with for 10 years.

Opportunities:

- James has obtained a new job, which means he has more finances to invest.
- James' financial advisor doesn't regularly follow up with him, so James is questioning whether or not to stay with the same firm. He wants to ensure he has enough money for retirement, that his children's educational funds are still on track for when they graduate, and how he can save money on his taxes.

How James feels:

- James has a few questions, but doesn't feel like his current advisor actually cares about his needs because the advisor rarely follows up.
- He's afraid that he's missing out on how to properly save on his taxes and he's secretly afraid appearing "stupid" with some of his questions.
- James feels very vulnerable for appearing like he doesn't know much about investments and is looking for a trusted resource he can feel comfortable with.

How is James finding a solution (client journey)?

- James has started to research various resources for what he should be doing. He has Googled "How To Invest Your Money" for some basic facts, but is still overwhelmed with what to do next.
- James reads articles about investments as they come into his LinkedIn feed.
- James uses his cell phone for a quick check of his emails. He uses his laptop when he's travelling, and takes it with him on weekends away with his family.
- He uses his office desktop for most of his work and it's where he usually logs into LinkedIn.
- On the golf course last week, James asked his friends about their financial planners and who his buddies work with.

What does James need to change from the current solution he has now?

- James needs to feel that the advisor he's going to work with understands his needs.
- He doesn't want to be sold, but just wants some advice about what he should be doing so he doesn't feel foolish.

- James wants to work with someone who has experience and has had a lot of prior success. He also wants someone who is approachable, who puts James' needs first, and someone James feels he can trust.

How to be the perfect solution for James and lead him through the sales funnel:

A few months ago, you reached out to connect with James on LinkedIn because he is connected to your client Lisa Brown, who is the CEO of her own consultancy.

You asked Lisa to make a "warm introduction" to James and when you sent your connection request, you acknowledged that Lisa has been a client of yours for many years, and offered to connect for a coffee sometime.

James has noticed you've been publishing articles about investing and financial planning in your LinkedIn status updates, and Lisa mentioned on the golf course that she was very pleased with how you've been managing her accounts.

When James recently updated his LinkedIn profile about his new job, you received a notification and sent him a private message that read:

> *"Hi James.*
>
> *We recently connected through Lisa Brown.*
>
> *I wanted to reach out and say CONGRATULATIONS on your new role at ABC Hotels!*
>
> *If you're interested in an introduction, my friend Phil McIntosh is looking for a new partner when it comes to his company's meeting facilities. I'd be happy to introduce you both if you'd like.*
>
> *In the meantime, I thought you may be interested in reading this article about financial planning and finding ways to save on your taxes: 'Safe Investments With High Returns Demystified' from Forbes.com www.forbes.com/demystified.'*
>
> *Let me know if I can help you with that introduction!"*

You followed up with a hand-written card to congratulate him on his new role, and also suggested you get together for a cup of coffee if he has any questions about his wealth management.

You'll notice that this exercise didn't start off with a pitch from the get-go, right?

The sales relationship was nurtured by:

- Positioning yourself as a thought-leader through status updates and posts.
- A referral and introduction from Lisa.
- Getting to know James and understanding both his problems and his deepest fears.
- Proactively reaching out with solutions and providing value before you ask for the sale: you offered a valuable article and suggested an introduction that could be mutually-beneficial to both Phil and James.

This process was also followed up with an unexpected handwritten card and another offer to get together.

This process applies to any type of sales and marketing. Give value first. Be consistent, but not pushy. Let your prospective client know you're interested in collaborating with them to find solutions and build trust for every step of their journey.

EXERCISE #8: CONSTRUCTING YOUR IDEAL CLIENT'S STORY

TIME COMMITMENT: 90+ MINUTES

Now it's your turn. Include as much information as you can, being sure to concentrate on their objections and deepest fears.

To make this process even more personalized, you may even want to Google an image of this fictitious person, so that when you are constructing your sales material, you feel that you are connecting directly with that persona.

Client:

_____

_____

Role:

_____

_____

Challenge:

_____

_____

Opportunities:

_____

_____

How the prospect feels:

_____

_____

The process they go through to find a solution:

_____

_____

What needs to change so the prospect moves from their current solution:

_____

_____

_____

How you're the perfect solution:

_____

_____

_____

_____

_____

_____

_____

_____

_____

_____

_____

_____

_____

_____

_____

_____

_____

_____

_____

_____

_____

_____

_____

_____

_____

_____

_____

_____

_____

_____

_____

LESSON #9

CREATE YOUR PROFESSIONAL PRESENCE USING LINKEDIN

"Become the person who would attract the results you seek."

~Jim Cathcart

According to BrandYourself.com[22], LinkedIn ranks higher than all other profiles when someone Googles your name.

LinkedIn allows you to:

- Obtain inbound leads, as prospective clients are actively searching for solutions that you provide.
- "Humanize" your brand.

- Extend your messaging to a qualified audience.
- Grow your professional network and gain followers for you and your company.
- Build thought leadership.
- Identify new opportunities and convert higher-paying clients.
- Attract more qualified talent for your company.

Some top statistics about LinkedIn and sales:

- LinkedIn is 277% more effective at converting clients than Facebook or Twitter.[24]
- 94% of B2B buyers report that they conduct some form of online research before purchasing a business product.[25]
- 98% of sales reps with more than 5000 LinkedIn connections meet or surpass quota.[26]

LinkedIn is no longer a want-to-have in your marketing toolkit, it's a *must* have.

If you aren't investing in telling your brand story and connecting with prospective clients, you should be. Your competition certainly is.

HOW LINKEDIN WORKS

LinkedIn was co-founded in May 2003 by Reid Hoffman, Allen Blue, Jean-Luc Vaillant, and Konstantin Guericke. (Fun Fact: LinkedIn was one of the very first social websites, even before Facebook was launched!)

More than just a resume site, LinkedIn members can:

- Include an "elevator pitch" of themselves in the Summary section.
- Provide descriptions of their company, their current position, and past positions.

- Connect with colleagues, prospects, clients.
- Obtain business opportunities.
- Engage and nurture professional relationships by "liking," sharing and/or commenting on each other's updates, and new job announcements.
- Post status updates and blog posts.
- Feature their most important skills and receive endorsements for those skills.
- Obtain testimonials and give testimonials with their network.

Like an online Rolodex, your network on LinkedIn is made up of your 1st-, 2nd-, and 3rd- degree connections.

1st-degree connections: LinkedIn members you've connected with. You have either accepted their invitation to connect, or they have accepted yours.

2nd-degree connections: LinkedIn members who are connected to your 1st-degree connections.

3rd-degree connections: LinkedIn members that aren't connected to you or your connections.

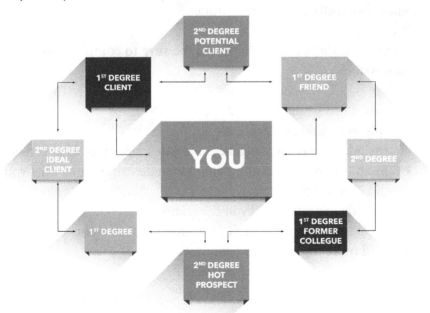

GETTING STARTED ON LINKEDIN

If you do not have a LinkedIn profile yet, hop to it! Visit www.linkedin.com and create a professional profile.

You will be asked for some basic personal information, including your name, email address, location, current employer, and where you went to college/university.

The wizard will prompt you to complete the rest of the sections.

A thorough LinkedIn profile is ideal for you and your brand. Be sure to focus on these three key areas: your image, your headline, and your summary first.

> Pro Tip: you don't have to complete it all in one sitting, nor do you have to complete every section.

Include as much information as you feel comfortable with. Remember: this is *your* story, and you can update it at any time!

Over time, your goal is to get to the "All Star" level using the LinkedIn "thermometer," because LinkedIn states that "members with complete profiles obtain 40x more opportunities.[26]"

To get to a 100% complete profile, be sure to complete the following:

- Add a profile picture.
- Add your industry & location.
- Include your current position and a description of what you do.
- Include two past positions along with descriptions of what you did in those past roles.
- Include any education you completed.
- Include 3 or more skills (I recommend focusing on 10-15).
- Add more than 50 connections.

THE IMPORTANCE OF KEYWORDS

When you are including information on your LinkedIn profile, your first priority is to write for the reader. So put yourself in their shoes. You already know what you do. Your goal is to persuade the reader to take action. You want to dazzle them with your expertise and want them to take action by contacting you and/or visiting your website.

Re-visit your ideal client avatar exercise to ensure you include certain words or phrases that align with your target audience. This is also helpful for optimizing your ranking within LinkedIn's search results.

LinkedIn's algorithm favors the use of keywords in the following sections

- Name
- Headline
- Summary
- Current Position
- Past Positions
- Anchor text in web links
- Skills

Be careful not to "keyword stuff" (i.e. repeating the same word over and over just for the sake of repetition). It's more important that you write for the reader instead of focusing on covering all the keywords.

THE THREE MOST IMPORTANT AREAS YOU NEED TO FOCUS ON NOW:

While there are many sections on LinkedIn to complete, the three-*most* important areas to complete are your photo, your headline, and your Summary.

I've done a lot of research on how to write a proper LinkedIn profiles, and I can safely say that most people haven't completed these three essential steps. (Even some key people who work at LinkedIn haven't completed these areas!)

When anyone visits your profile, these are the three areas that capture the most attention. If they like what they see, and are looking for more information about you, they will dive a little deeper to look at the other sections. If not, they move on.

KEY AREA #1: YOUR PROFESSIONAL PHOTO

Like it or not, your facial appearance plays a major role when people judge your personality traits.

According to researchers at Princeton University[23], it only takes 100 milliseconds for someone to form an impression of you just by looking at a photo of your face.

Ensure you are looking warmly into the camera, smiling, and wearing appropriate professional attire. You want to appear confident, approachable, and trustworthy. The photo should be cropped to feature only your head and shoulders so that it's close enough to see your face.

THE DON'TS

I've seen a lot of horrible profile photos on LinkedIn including the following "Do *Not* dos":

Don't Pretend to be George Clooney

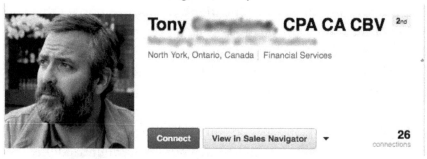

Even if this person looks a lot like George Clooney, this is not an appropriate LinkedIn photo. He's not looking at the camera, he's not smiling, and he's not dressed in business attire. What this person's profile tells me: he's not interested in obtaining new business or investing in his online presence.

74

Don't Use an Avatar

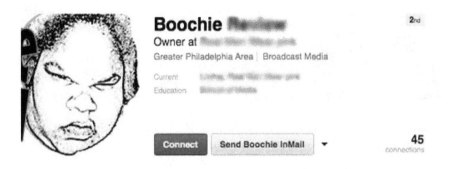

This is just a sketch of the person; I'm a little scared to see what the real "Boochie" looks like!

Don't Be a Logo

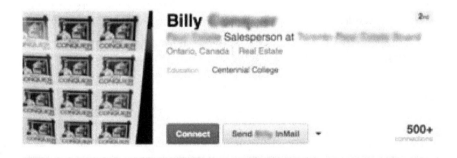

People want to connect with people: they don't want to connect with a logo. When you plan to meet someone face-to-face, they will often go to LinkedIn to see what you look like before you meet.

I've also seen LinkedIn profile photos that have included images of garlic, pets, and babies. Don't ever do this!

Clothing is Mandatory!

Yes, this is an actual photo from LinkedIn. I don't think this person would show up to a business meeting without a shirt on, so it would be in his best interest to invest in a professional headshot.

Other suggested "Do *Not* Dos":

- Passport photos
- Images that include other people
- Images with people cropped out of it
- Photos that are pixellated
- Outdated photos
- Images taken at events, including weddings or other celebrations
- Images with a "duck face," "selfies," or wearing sunglasses
- "Glamour shots" from the 1980s.

THE DO'S

The following are some examples of great profile pictures:

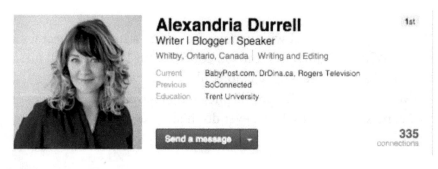

Alexandria's photos shows her smiling warmly and she appears confident, professional and approachable.

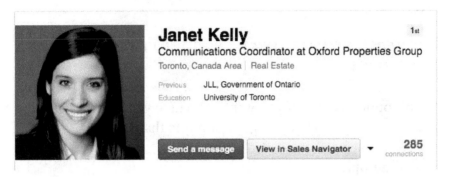

Janet Kelly 1st

Communications Coordinator at Oxford Properties Group

Toronto, Canada Area | Real Estate

Previous JLL, Government of Ontario

Education University of Toronto

Send a message | View In Sales Navigator ▾

285 connections

Similarly, Janet is also well-dressed, with a beautiful smile. She's dressed professionally and appears very confident.

Best practices for choosing the perfect professional photo:

- Invest in a professional photographer who will capture you in the best light.
- If you cannot afford a professional, at least have your photo taken against a plain background using natural lighting.
- Make eye contact with the camera.
- Smile warmly (ideally show your teeth).
- Dress professionally.
- Crop the image so that it focuses on your head and shoulders.

KEY AREA #2: YOUR HEADLINE

Located directly beneath your name, and right beside your photo, is the area for your LinkedIn headline. You have 120 characters to define who you are and how you help your audience.

By default, LinkedIn will include your current title, but does your title really have any value for your prospective clients? For example, my title is "Principal of PUNCH!media": that doesn't let anyone who I am, what I do, or who I work with.

You can write your LinkedIn headline as a sentence to include your unique value proposition, or you can use keywords to define who you are.

OPTION A: YOUR HEADLINE WRITTEN AS A SENTENCE

This option is ideal if you want to include your specialization or niche. You may also have a tagline or motto that fits well.

For example:

Forensic Accountant: helping corporate lawyers quantify damages with business valuations and forensic accounting.

I'm very fond of Sue Horner's LinkedIn headline:

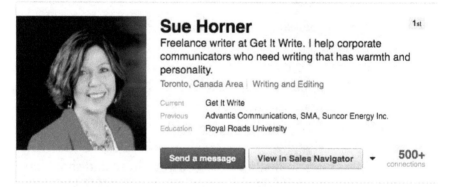

"I help corporate communicators who need writing that has warmth and personality." Certainly tells more of a story than just "freelance writer," doesn't it?

HEADLINE FORMULAS

Helping _____ to _____
   (target audience)   (results you deliver)

-or-

Specializing in _____ for _____
    (results)   (target audience)

OPTION B: KEYWORD-FOCUSED HEADLINE

You can see that Nate's focus is "Social Selling" and his niche is working with financial professionals. He's used keywords and his niche to tell his "story."

Like Nate, I also use keywords in my headline. I wear many "hats" and wanted to be sure I focus on the most important roles that I have. I've highlighted my niche as a LinkedIn Trainer, and I also threw in a little "social proof" of having been called a "Social Media Guru" by CBC radio because it makes a great first impression!

Note: I have seen some people use checkmarks, stars, and other bullets to "jazz" up their profile. I don't like them. To me, "jazzy" isn't professional. If you are going to use bullets, keep them simple bullets (like the ones you see in my headline.)

KEY AREA #3: YOUR SUMMARY

Your Summary on LinkedIn is *the* focal point of your profile. It is an opportunity to properly position yourself as an expert. Think of this section as an "elevator pitch."

You have 2,000 characters to cover who you are, what you do, and how you help your audience. Be sure to let yourself shine.

Remember this is *your* story to tell, so use your language. Be mindful of what's in it for reader and write the copy *they* want to know about you.

As a word of caution, it often takes me between 5 to 10 hours to write a comprehensive summary for the executives I work with.

Your story will continue to change as you move through your career. The good news is Linkedin can- and should be—changed over time.

Top Tips:

- Write the copy in a MS Word document so you can manage your character count.
- Ensure the copy is easy-to-read on the screen. Include blocks of information instead of long paragraphs of text.
- Write your summary in 1st person (I am) instead of 3rd person ("Joe Smith is..."). It's more compelling for the reader and allows you to frame how passionate you are about what you do. Lead with a powerful first sentence, whether or not it's a tagline, or frame your story emotionally. Your goal is to get the reader interested in finding out more about you.
- Include your accomplishments. If you're afraid of coming across like you're bragging, simply describe how passionate you are. This way, you look like you're committed to what you do and everyone wants to work with someone who *loves* what they do! Besides, on LinkedIn, you're *supposed* to include all your "wins" and accomplishments. That's what this channel is for!

Be sure to cover:

- Why do you do what you do?
- What kinds of clients do you work with?
- How long have you been working within your field of work?
- What makes you unique?
- What are the key accomplishments you are proudest of?

Dovetail in your company story:

- What does your company do? How do you help your target audience?
- What is the core value and mission of your company?
- Can you pull in a quote or testimonial from another source?

Include a call-to-action:

- How can people contact you (email/phone) or what is the next step you want them to take?

When I write profiles for executives, I tend to use the Summary section focus on *who you are*. I use the Current Position section to focus on your role and *what you do* at your organization.

EXERCISE #9: LINKEDIN SUMMARY WORKSHEET

TIME COMMITMENT: 4+ HOURS

The following is an easy-to-follow "plug & play" worksheet you can use as a guide for creating your LinkedIn Summary.

As the _____, with over _____
        (insert your current position)
years of experience at _____,
               (company or industry)
I believe in _____.
               (your core values)
I understand the challenges of _____
             (problem your target audience is having)
and I'm passionate about delivering _____.
               (solution)
Some of my noteworthy accomplishments include:

_____

_____

_____

_____

_____

In my past position as _____at
               (past role)
_____, I was responsible
        (past company)
for_____ and
          (responsibilities)
achieved_____. The mission for
          (achievements)
_____is _____.
    (company I work for)   (mission statement)

We specialize in:

_____

_____

_____

_____

_____

On a personal side, I enjoy _____.

(hobbies/interests)

LINKEDIN SUMMARY EXAMPLE #1:
MARKETING DIRECTOR (1576 CHARACTERS)

I am the Marketing Director at FashionStores Inc., one of the leading plus-sized fashion retailers in US and Canada. Our mission is to deliver high quality, fashionable, affordable clothing to a discerning audience.

During the past five years at FashionStores, I've successfully launched "The Buyers Circle" and have been responsible for overseeing all aspects of business planning, product conceptualization, and integrated marketing campaigns to our 1,000 stores. During this time, we have seen a 20% increase in market share.

I am driven to help ensure our target audience of women ages 35-55 are eager to come to our stores and have an excellent shopping experience.

It's important that we listen to our audience, both at the store level and through our social media channels. I believe our ongoing commitment to customer service is the key to our company's growth and profitability.

During my five years working at HomeStore, I worked collaboratively with the Sales Director to develop and implement sales initiatives to aid in new business development and customer retention. I was responsible for a $4M budget.

My noteworthy accomplishments include:
- Board of Directors for Children's Charity.
- Volunteer Marketing Director for Fashion Association's annual ball.
- Increasing corporate market share for FashionStores in 2012.
- Bachelor of Arts from The University of Marketing.
- MBA from The Elite School of Business.

If you would like to connect with me, please send me a personalized note via LinkedIn or email me at janesmith@fashionstores.com

LINKEDIN SUMMARY EXAMPLE #2:
FINANCIAL ADVISOR (1481 CHARACTERS)

My role as Financial Advisor is to start by listening first. Whatever your goals and dreams are, I use my 20+ years of experience and knowledge of money management to create a thorough plan for your future.

I love helping people get a clear picture of their future by mapping out their current financial status and developing a clear strategy based on their goals and objectives. I gain a great deal of satisfaction when my clients achieve their financial goals and are able to build a legacy for their family.

Getting involved in the financial services industry was a natural transition for me. My father was a Financial Advisor, and I saw how he was able to transform people's lives by simplifying the most complex tax and legal structures so his clients could understand their plans. My father is not only my role model, but my mentor as well.

Family is extremely important to me, and I feel that many of my clients are my extended family. I'm proud to have been trusted with the financial affairs of families over several generations.

Our company specializes in:
- Retirement planning
- Estate planning
- Pension planning
- Investment & financial planning services
- Wealth management strategies

We schedule regular meetings with you to make sure you are on track with your retirement.

Email me at billsmith@yourcompany or call me at (647) 555-9876 if you want to connect or have any questions.

HERE ARE SOME OTHER KEY SECTIONS ON LINKEDIN THAT YOU SHOULD COMPLETE (OVER TIME)

Obtain Your Custom URL (aka Hotlink)

By default, LinkedIn will give you a long URL that looks like:

linkedin.com/in/firstnamelastname012-3456

Customize your "vanity" URL so that it looks more polished on your profile. List just your first name and last name so it reads:

linkedin.com/in/yourname

Add your "vanity" URL to your email signature and include it on your business cards to extend your reach and encourage people to connect with you. If your "vanity" URL is taken, you may have to add a middle initial or reverse the order so that it's your surname, then your first name.

Customize Contact Info Section

You can customize up to three web links in the "Contact info" area of your profile. Customize your copy by choosing the "other" field in the dropdown menu. Add your phone number, your Twitter handle (optional,) and your mailing address (optional.)

Add A Second Email Address

I recommend that you add a second email address (i.e. your "home" email address.) By doing this, you will still be able to access your LinkedIn account even if you lose access to your work account. It looks more professional to use your work email address as the primary, public version, but whichever email address you choose as your primary account will be the one to receive all notifications from LinkedIn.

Add Multimedia (PowerPoints & Videos)

Adding a visual element to your profile (including videos or photos) provides the reader with a more dynamic experience. Include a version of your brochure or portfolio into a PowerPoint presentation. Include a video bio about yourself and/or your company.

Add Your Experience

For your current position or any past position, you have 2,000 characters for each section.

Be as specific as possible with your deliverables for each position and the results you generated.

Since every person who works for your organization is a brand ambassador, I recommend that your organization provide everyone with a consistent paragraph about what your company does and how you help your clients.

Add Your Education & Accomplishments

- Where did you attend school?
- Years attended (optional).
- Field of study (optional).
- Activities, Societies (optional).

Add Skills

The Skills section is linked to the endorsements section. When people endorse you, it's usually because you (or LinkedIn) have indicated these are your top skills.

- You need at least 3 skills to get to 100% completion.
- Focus on your top 10-15 skills.
- You can add up to 50 skills total.
- You can delete skills that are not relevant to what you do.
- You may wish to repeat similar keywords. For example, I include Marketing, Social Media Marketing, Digital Marketing, and so on. They may seem redundant, but from a keyword perspective, this helps you rank higher when someone searches that particular set of words.

Add Projects

List specific projects you've worked on, and the key people who participated with you in these projects. You can also use this field to highlight any public speaking you've done, or other areas that you can't categorize in the other sections.

Add Languages

If you speak additional languages, include them in this section along with your proficiency.

Add Publications

In this section you can include any articles you've written or if you have been featured in any publications. You can also hotlink online articles from your LinkedIn profile to the news source.

Add Organizations

List your membership activity. Do you belong to a Board of Trade or Chamber of Commerce? What about an industry association? Perhaps you sit on a Board of Directors?

Add Honors & Awards

This is a great section to highlight your successes! These honors and awards may be yours or one received by your company.

Add Certifications

Even though some of your certifications may be industry-specific and your target audience doesn't know what they mean, it's important to include them to highlight the investment you've made to your education. Highlight any certifications you've completed and the regulating boards who have awarded you with the designation.

Add Courses

Similar to Certifications, highlight any relevant professional development courses you've completed.

Add Volunteering & Causes

Highlight some of the charities you're involved in, or have been involved with in the past. Include a description of what these causes do.

> Pro Tip: This a great area to focus on for students and new graduates who don't have a lot of work experience but want to highlight some of their volunteer experience.

Add Additional Info (optional)

You may wish to include some personal information about yourself in this section. I find this information to be helpful for "conversation starters" or "icebreakers."

You can decide whether or not you want to include information about your family. For industries such as insurance or financial planning, including your personal information can build resonance with your target audience. For other industries, this information may be irrelevant.

You may wish to include your proudest non-working accomplishments such as running marathons, or "searching for your city's best burger" (I like that one a lot.) Again, it's *your* story to tell.

Do *not* publish your year of birth or your home address. This isn't for vanity purposes, but because this information could be used for fraudulent purposes (and isn't necessarily professional either.)

> Pro Tip: I also *highly* recommend you do not publish, click on, or engage with non-professional posts. This may include math questions, "what is the first word you see" posts or personal announcements.

LinkedIn is not Facebook. When I see my connections engage with these kinds of posts, I wonder if they actually spend time working, or are they just wasting time?

In the "Additional Info" section, you may want to include:

- Hobbies and interests.
- Listing your contact information again.
- The "legal disclaimer" copy (if you're in a compliance-based industry.)

LESSON #10

GET "SOCIAL PROOF" VIA TESTIMONIALS

"It takes many good deeds to build a good reputation, and only one bad one to lose it."

~Benjamin Franklin

Having a happy client acknowledge your competency and proficiency is a wonderful way to obtain "social proof."

According to Dr. Robert Cialdini's book *Influence: The Psychology of Persuasion*, "social proof" is described as:

> "When people are uncertain about a course of action, they tend to look to those around them to guide their decisions and actions. They especially want to know what everyone else is doing – especially their peers."[28]

In other words, if someone is willing to stake their professional reputation on you to say how awesome you are, then other people are more likely to trust you as well.

According to a 2013 LinkedIn study, customer testimonials and case studies are considered the two most effective content marketing tactics.[29]

You've probably done this kind of research yourself. You've likely used Travelocity.com or another review site to research other people's opinions about a vacation spot, product, service, or brand. You probably have trusted the review, even if you don't know the person who wrote it!

According to Searchengineland.com:

- 88% have read reviews to determine the quality of a local business.
- 39% read reviews on a regular basis.
- 72% of consumers say that positive reviews make them trust a local business more.[29]

It's great if you can obtain a testimonial from a client or former client who fits the description of your ideal client. You should also obtain testimonials from your professional superiors or your staff to highlight your leadership skills. Or, you can simply ask someone you know to provide you with a character reference.

As long as the person who provides it is trustworthy, a testimonial is one of the strongest pieces of information on your LinkedIn profile.

There are two ways you can obtain a testimonial:

OPTION #1. GIVE A TESTIMONIAL AND GET A TESTIMONIAL

By the law of reciprocity (from Dr. Robert Cialidini's book: *Influence: The Psychology of Persuasion,*) if you do something nice for someone, they usually feel compelled to do something nice in return.

When you write testimonial for one of your connections, LinkedIn will invite the recipient to return the favor. (In my experience, the recipient will reciprocate about 50% of the time.)

OPTION #2. JUST ASK

If you've done great work for a vendor, or if you know someone who can provide you with a character reference, simply reach out and ask.

I recommend you do the heavy lifting and write the copy for the person. This way, they will be much more likely to comply. (If you've ever had to write a testimonial, you know how time consuming it can be.)

Some people may prefer to write it themselves, but if you provide them with pre-written copy, you can let them know the areas and skills you want to focus on.

Dear (name),

I'm in the process of updating my LinkedIn profile, and would love to include a testimonial from you. To make this process easier, I have written some draft copy below. Please feel free to change or re-write any of the copy to ensure it fits your voice.

It would be great to have your feedback before next Friday. Let me know if you have any questions.

Thank you in advance.

Kindly yours,

(Your name)

Pro Tip: Modify the copy for each person so you don't have the exact same testimonial repeated.

A general outline for the testimonial may be similar to:

I have had the pleasure of working with (your name) for over _____ years. During this time, s/he helped me _____(include some of the issues or problems you helped to solve).

I have always found (your name) to be _____(include your experience with him). I would recommend (your name) to anyone who needs assistance in (delivering the results you provide).

EXERCISE #10: GATHER SOCIAL PROOF

TIME COMMITMENT: 30+ MINUTES

Your next step is to reach out to at least five connections to give and/or get a testimonial.

It may be helpful for you to write down the following information before you reach out:

- Name and contact information.
- How long have you known this person?
- What was the problem you needed to solve for this person?
- How did you solve their problem?
- Was the situation unique? How so?
- How long do they have to respond to your request?

_____
_____
_____
_____
_____
_____
_____
_____
_____
_____
_____
_____
_____
_____
_____
_____

BONUS Q & A SECTION:

I'm often asked the following questions and I wanted to be sure I covered off the following information:

Question #1: How much is *too* much on your LinkedIn profile?

Answer #1: According to LinkedIn, having a complete profile will provide you with 40x more opportunities, so be sure to include as many details as you like can as long as it's relevant to your brand.

Here are my thoughts about how much copy you should include:

The Goldilocks Rule: Not too much, not too little. Just right.

Write the copy for the reader. Think about their perspective and make it compelling for them. You don't want to maximize the character count just because you can; you want to make sure you include *important* information. In my Summary, I have maxed out my 2,000-character count (I have a lot to say.)

Long copy answers objections (and can build rapport.)

Most people skim when they are reading copy. If they want more information, you want to be sure they are able to find the answers. You never know: that hobby that you included on your profile might just be the #1 reason your client reaches out! According to Dr. Charles Edwards, long time Dean of Retailing at New York University, "The more facts you tell, the more you sell.[31]"

Include variations of your keywords.

Using variations of the same keywords in your Summary, your Current Position, Skills etc. allows you to cover all your bases when your target audience is searching for you. Keywords affect search engine optimization (SEO). For example, I include: Digital Marketing, Social Media Marketing, Social Media, Social Marketing, Marketing. While these terms may seem redundant, people may prefer to use one term when they are searching for a solution.

Question #2: Should I invest in a Premium Account on LinkedIn?
Answer #2: It depends on why you want to invest in a Premium account.

There are various levels of Premium Accounts, including LinkedIn Professional, Job Seeker, Recruiter Lite, and Sales Navigator.

Each Premium Level has a different purpose and different monthly cost.

As a basic overview, Premium accounts allow you to:

- Access InMails (you can send emails without being connected on LinkedIn.)
- See more "Who's viewed your profile."
- Get deeper access to LinkedIn's search functionality.
- Set alerts for changes within your network or you can save searches.

The Premium accounts can be very beneficial – for people who *use* it. No matter which level you choose, you want to be sure that you get a return on your investment.

If you are in sales and are converting enough revenue per month to warrant the monthly investment, then I highly recommend it.

Similarly, if you're job hunting, there are many reasons to invest in the Premium account. (Be sure you have an up-to-date LinkedIn profile!)

LinkedIn will allow you to try the Premium account for a free month, so make sure your profile is rock-solid before you give it a whirl.

LESSON #11

CREATE THOUGHT LEADERSHIP AND DOMINATE YOUR NICHE

"The goal of business then should not be to simply sell to anyone who wants what you have, but rather to find people who believe what you believe"[32]

~Simon Sinek

As I've already mentioned, thanks to social media, you are a brand. You are also media agency. Your voice of authority is essential to help you build your reputation and dominate your niche.

Creating compelling content is the "heavy lifting" of social media. It takes time, but it's one of the most essential elements of any marketing strategy.

Providing your perspective and answering questions creates an opportunity for you to stand out amongst your competition. Publishing compelling content will help to build rapport and trust. It can also help you to rank higher in Search Engine Optimization (SEO), and since most of us use Google when we are searching for solutions, your post could be the first point of contact on your prospect's path to purchase.

Building thought leadership by publishing content on social media is important because:

- 88% of technology buyers said thought leadership was important or critical in determining a shortlist of vendors.[33]
- It costs 75% less to generate leads via social media than any other channel.[34]
- 79% of would-be buyers say thought leadership is critical for determining which companies they want to learn more about.[35]
- Whether you're publishing via blogs, newsletters, or videos, you will showcase your deep understanding about your industry and reassure the reader that you know what you're doing.

YOUR CONTENT STRATEGY

Quality content trumps quantity *every* time. You want to *earn* your audience's attention by sharing the right information at the right time.

You want to ensure your content is relevant to the channel and it's relevant to the reader. If it's not relevant, it won't resonate.

One of the easiest ways to save time and eliminate overwhelm is to develop a content calendar to outline what you're going to post, when you're going to post the content, and the channel(s) you plan to share it with.

Having an action plan will help you to stay aligned with your goals and will allow you to tailor your content so that it becomes more compelling and strategic.

Here's how to get your content strategy started:

Step #1: Do an audit of your existing material.

Look to your existing marketing material. Most organizations already have content that can be expanded upon, or reduced with a bit of editing. Can you use any of the content you've already assembled and re-purpose it?

Step #2: Take a look at the social media channels of your competition and your industry at large

Audit the online landscape to assess your opportunities. What can you provide that your competition is not? Are there industry statistics you can share with your audience? Think outside the box! Can you look at other industries and "twist" them? (I learned this cool concept from Julie Cottineau's Brand School — www.brandschoolonline.com.)

For example, how can your brand "twist" principles, emotions or concepts from one market or company and make it apply to your brand? How can you make your brand "the happiest place on earth" (Disney)? Or, what principles can you apply from "It's everywhere you want to be" (VISA)?

Step #3: Start to craft some compelling content

- Think of a new perspective to solve a particular problem for your audience.
- Write about challenges you've faced and how you overcame them (case studies etc.)
- Talk about common misconceptions about your industry.
- Share upcoming trends that haven't reached the masses yet.
- Forecast what your industry is going to look like in 5, 10, 15 years.
- Ask your audience "What's one question you're challenged with right now?"
- If you work for a large organization, feature an employee, board member, and/or client.
- Take a behind-the-scenes look at your company.
- Share step-by-step do-it-yourself tips (they will come to you for the heavy lifting anyway.)

- Highlight your involvement with local events or your favorite charity.
- Can you "news jack" on current trends?
- If it works within the right context, include an inspirational quote that resonates with your audience.

> Pro Tip: Make sure you do *not* use content about someone's death, such as "10 Things We Learned About Robin William's Suicide." This is horrible marketing.

I often write blog posts based on a recent question a client has asked me about. I figure, if one person has that question, then there are several others who also have the same question, but are too shy to ask.

GRAB ATTENTION USING CAPTIVATING HEADLINES

"On the average, five times as many people read the headline as read the body copy. When you have written your headline, you have spent eighty cents out of your dollar.[36]"-David Ogilvy

Whether you're sharing status updates, posting blog headlines, deploying emails, or tweeting, your goal is to grab someone's attention so they're interested in reading more.

For copy to be effective, you want to:

- Resonate emotionally. (Fear, anger, and humor are trigger emotions that connect quickly and effectively.) Surprisingly, negative words/superlatives perform 30% better than positive ones.[37]
- Focus on what's in it for them (the audience.)
- Add urgency.

Look at magazine covers, newspaper or online headlines for examples of ways you can capture your audiences' attention. At Weddingbells

Magazine, the editors decided to publish a cover that only had the title of the magazine and a beautiful image of a bride. This aesthetically-pleasing cover didn't convert as high on the newsstands as our other cover images had. It seems we consumers believe we get more value when we see many calls-to-action including "101 Ways To Get Your Bikini Body Ready Without A Sit Up."

These kinds of headlines can sometimes be misleading to the core message of the post, but a "meh" headline won't get anyone's attention.

Some of the best performing headlines include:

- How To_____
- The Easiest Way To _____
- Why You Need To_____
- Top X Ways To_____
- The Shocking Truth About _____
- What I Learned About _____
- Do You _____?
- Here's How To Fix _____
- Avoid Doing _____
- Why _____ Doesn't Work

The next time you send a tweet or write a headline, make it compelling and ensure it stands out.

Other top tips for creating content:

- Focus on one key message.
- Keep the copy simple and easy to understand.
- Make it "reader friendly" (i.e. write the way you speak.)
- Include your personality, but keep it professional.
- Think about specific keywords that work within your niche.
- Proofread your work. Typos are a big no-no.

Find ways to get your audience to engage (ask them questions and/or ask them to share the post with their network). Look at your metrics. From Google Analytics to LinkedIn statistics, measure which posts attract the most readers and see if you can decipher why that post worked better than others? Was it the content? Was it the time of day, or the day of the week? What were some of the key factors for its success? Try to replicate this success in the future.

IMAGES SAY 60,000 WORDS

You've probably heard the saying "an image says 1,000 words." It's not surprising that when copy is paired with visuals, 40% of people will respond better to visual information than plain text.[38]

This is because our brains process images 60,000 times faster than they do text.[39]

It's important to note, that while some images found in search engines such as Google, may be easily found online, but this doesn't mean they are free for you to use. Never assume that online images are free to use. Whenever necessary, obtain permission or purchase stock photography before using the image or photo.

Some tools you can use to help you create images, even when you don't know how to design include:

- Canva.com (my personal fave)
- Picmonkey.com
- BeFunky.com

These online photo editor services are fairly easy to use, and are an affordable (sometimes free!) resource if you don't have any designs skills.

Another option is to use video. Video blogging (aka, vlogging) can help to build even deeper resonance with your target audience. I find video marketing challenging because it takes longer to organize, film and edit, but I highly recommended vlogging as a key way to build your brand presence.

I cannot stress enough the importance of ensuring you share the right content in the right context.

Never mass blast your content to every social media channel. Each site has a unique purpose. LinkedIn is the professional network so it's important to maintain a professional presence here. Facebook is the "friends and family" network, so you can be a bit more casual with this audience (depending upon your brand, of course.) Twitter is a microblog limited to publishing content in under 140 characters. You don't want to share the same information on LinkedIn that you've uploaded to Snapchat. Ensure your content is customized properly.

> Pro Tip: You *can* use other channels as syndication to drive traffic back to your blog, but only if the messaging is deployed strategically.

LINKEDIN PUBLISHING PLATFORM AND STATUS UPDATES

Publishing content on LinkedIn is a great way to grow a professional audience.

I typically publish a blog post on my site first, and then use the same copy and upload it to LinkedIn's Publishing Platform. (You can do this by clicking on the "Publish a post" button on LinkedIn.)

I publish on my blog to drive traffic back to my site and for the audience that isn't on LinkedIn yet. Lately, I've found that I receive much more engagement and "social shares" on LinkedIn than the content I post on my site.

When you publish a blog post on LinkedIn, your connections will be sent a notification. When any of your 1st degree connections interact by liking or commenting on your post, the engagement of these connection may also reach your 2nd degree connections (if the engagement is seen in the 2nd degree connection's LinkedIn "feed".) Quite simply, your post could be seen by others beyond your network of connections.

One of my posts on LinkedIn was picked up by LinkedIn's content aggregator called Pulse, and was seen by over 13,000 people! You just never know what kind of material is going to resonate with your target audience (and beyond!)

I'm often asked how often should someone publish content on their LinkedIn profile and/or on their site. My goal is to publish at least one blog post per week, and two status updates.

That's what I love about LinkedIn. You don't have to be on this channel all the time to reap rewards.

I aim to be top-of-mind without being too annoying. Someone in my LinkedIn network publishes their posts every *hour*. This is too much content for LinkedIn and is better suited for Twitter. So this person doesn't dominate my "feed"; I've hidden all their posts and now I don't see *any* of their posts. Publishing too often is a detriment to your brand. People will either ignore what you post, hide your posts, or delete you from their network.

One final note. At the end of every blog post, include standard copy or your unique value proposition to highlight who you are (this often referred to as a boilerplate.)

The following is a boilerplate I use at the bottom of all my posts:

> Leslie Hughes is a LinkedIn Trainer, Profile Writer, Professor of Social Media, and Principal of PUNCH!media
>
> Leslie was called a "Social Media Guru" by CBC Radio and was featured on CTV's "The Social" discussing "How To Manage Your Digital Identity." Leslie has been working in digital marketing since 1997 and founded PUNCH!media in 2009. PUNCH!media clients include The Children's Wish Foundation of Canada, Guardian Life Insurance Company of America and TVO.

PUNCH!media's goal is to empower through education and help executives gain confidence in their online presence so you convert higher-paying clients.

This way, if this is the first time the reader is exposed to your post, they can find you and obtain more information.

To create your "boilerplate," revisit Exercise #3 and construct your unique value proposition.

EXERCISE #11: BOOST YOUR ONLINE PRESENCE THROUGH THOUGHT LEADERSHIP

TIME COMMITMENT: 1+ HOURS PER MONTH TO ORGANIZE, WRITE POSTS AND DEPLOY CONTENT.

Let's get you organized with your very own content strategy:

Step #1: Grab a calendar or open an MS Excel file.

Step #2: Write down the dates of the events you are involved with throughout the year.

Include your involvement at charity events, open houses, VIP events, conferences, or even when new announcements are made.

Step #3: Develop content to highlight your involvement with these events.

Can you create buzz ahead of time? Reframe your "brags" with how passionate you are. Don't over-promote: there is a fine balance between self-promotion and annoying your connections. (I use the principle of "do unto others.")

Step #4: Think about content themes you can write about. These can be monthly, weekly, or daily themes.

You know your industry and the peaks and valleys of when business gets busy. Build momentum ahead of time.

For example, do you notice the "Back To School" promotions start in early August, and Christmas promotions begin right after Hallowe'en (or Thanksgiving if you're in the US)? There is a build up to the "big event." How can you build up to your peak times or main events?

You may wish to look at your entire year at-a-glance for themes. Some themes can be date-specific (International left-handers day) or monthly themes that coincide with:

January: New Years Day. Martin Luther King Day (US).
February: Valentines' Day.
March: St. Patrick's Day.
April: First day of Spring.
May: Mother's Day. Victoria Day (Canada). Memorial Day (US).
June: Father's Day. First day of summer.
July: Canada Day. (Canada) Independence Day (US).
August: Civic Day (Canada).
September: Back to School. Labor Day. First day of Fall.
October: Hallowe'en. Thanksgiving (Canada). Columbus Day (US).
November: Thanksgiving (US).
December: First day of Winter. Christmas, and many other religious holidays.

Step #5: Fill in your publishing slots.

Then, schedule your posts weekly, and by date. Publish often enough that you're consistently top-of-mind, but not too much to annoy your audience.

You also don't want to overcommit by sharing a ton of information too fast, because you'll want to be able to sustain your writing over time.

To keep things simple with your LinkedIn status updates and/or tweets, you can also curate content (re-share) from other sources. Think about what kind of content is interesting to your target audience. Align the content you're publishing with your audience's hobbies or interests.

For certain audiences you may wish to share posts about golf, marathon running, tennis, skiing, wine tasting, etc.

Before you post, always ask yourself:

- Is this the kind of quality content my audience wants to see?
- Does this content fit with my brand?

Step #6: Fill in your publishing slots.

I'll often write a few blog posts in one sitting so they are ready well in advance of the publishing date. This is excellent for video blogs (vlogs) as well. You can record several videos in one session, and then stagger the days you publish them.

Another time-saving tip is to repeat your posts. Just because it's "old news" to you, it may be "new news" to people in your network. Content is not always seen by your entire network the first time you share it, so strategically share the same article (as long as you provide enough time in between each post). For example, at Weddingbells magazine many of the travel articles about honeymoons were repeated every two or three years. The cycle for brides would turn over by that time, and we could include the same content to a fresh set of eyes.

Step #7: Find ways to syndicate your content.

At the end of your post, invite people to share: "*If you found this information interesting, please share it with your network.*" Tweet the headline of your post with a link to the URL. Find other media outlets that will also share your content.

> Pro Tip: If you are in a compliance-based industry, you must ensure your Compliance Officer approves all copy ahead of time. This is another reason why you should have your copy developed in advance!

Step #8: Measure your metrics

Look at which posts worked, and which posts did not perform as well. What were the variables?

DEEP THOUGHTS ABOUT CREATING YOUR BRAND

Digital anthropologist and author Brian Solis coined the term "Digital Darwinism." He says we are living in *"a time when technology and society are evolving faster than the ability of many organizations to adapt."*[40] He also states that *"no business is too big to fail or too small to succeed."*

Did you ever think that companies like Polaroid or Blockbuster would have ever filed for bankruptcy? Could you ever have conceptualized that companies like Airbnb or Uber would have cannibalized the hotel or taxi industry without owning any property or cars?

Bob Dylan may have written this song in 1964, but the words are still applicable today:

> "Come gather 'round people where ever you roam
> And admit that the waters around you have grown
> And accept it that soon you'll be drenched to the bone
> If your time to you is worth savin'
> Then you better start swimmin' or you'll sink like a stone,
> For the times they are a' changin'!"

You have to continuously be evolving to stay relevant in today's marketplace.

You know you're a rock star. If you haven't started yet, get started. If you *have* started branding yourself, it's time to kick it up a notch. There is *always* something you can do today to invest in your brand and presence for tomorrow.

No one has all the answers. Many of us are making it up as we go. It's time to put yourself out there, develop your brand, and share your message. Who knows? You could be the next YouTuber or famous blogger! Be consistent, be creative, and be confident in *You*: The brand.

The next step on your journey to success is to find the right ways to reach out and build a network of quality connections

Let's connect with confidence, shall we?

MODULE #2

CONNECT

"It's not what you know, but WHO you know."
~Unknown

"Show me your friends and I'll show you your future."
~John Kuebler

Making the right connections matters, and building your network is a *major* part of your social capital.

The right connections can help you propel your brand and your career.

In social media, it sometimes seems like we are sending our messages out into the ether. I often wonder if my messages are getting any traction when there is little response, but trust me, people *are* seeing your posts, whether or not they respond.

When I attended my high school reunion, I had quite a few people approach me who said "*I see your posts on LinkedIn! You're doing so well with your business. I see you've been speaking everywhere!*"

(I swear they thought I was the next Tony Robbins!)

I was a bit flabbergasted because none of these people had actually commented on any of my posts, so I had presumed my status updates and posts hadn't really been noticed.

Even though your messages are being sent from computer-to-computer, or device-to-device, we *are* fundamentally connecting human-to-human.

I believe that whether you are sending content or making connections, *quality* always trumps quantity. (I can't stress this belief enough: **quality always trumps quantity**.) About 99% of other LinkedIn trainers I've followed will say *"connect with everyone, because you never know where your next lead is going to come from."*

I wholeheartedly *disagree*. "Everyone" is not a strategy.

I believe it's much more important to deepen connections with your network instead of casting a wide net of loose connections.

I'll admit, the number of connections you have can sometimes be a bit of an "ego" game. It may seem like having a high number of followers is a good metric to strive for, but if none of those people are listening, then that metric doesn't mean a damned thing.

HOW TO BUILD

If I were to ask you, *"what is the #1 way you've built your brand and converted business?"* chances are you'd say "word-of-mouth," right?

Well, social media has been called "word-of-mouth on steroids."

The exponential growth of the "word-of-mouth" via social media is based on Metcalfe's Law[41], which can be generally described as:

"1) The number of possible cross-connections in a network grow as the square of the number of computers in the network increases.

2) The community value of a network grows as the square of the number of its users increase."

Other people argue that it's Zipf's Law that describes *"how in any system of resources there are a small number of items of very high frequency and value and a 'long tail' of many more of decreasing frequency and value. It is, in essence, an empirical description of hierarchical distribution of resources (i.e., rich get richer...)*[42]"

And just for giggles, here's one more confusing academic concept to throw at you: the "Dunbar Number," which states that the size of a meaningful and stable social group for humans is about 150 people. *"Beyond that size, additional members add diminishing value. But even within that 150 there is considerable range in affinity and sentiment.*[43]"

My brain hurts just trying to understand what all these theories really mean, but when I think about the potential reach via social media, I often refer to the 1980s television commercial featuring Heather Locklear where she says "and they told two friends, and so on, and so on and so on.[44]"

Your connections are more likely going to share your messages if they are relevant and if your content educates, entertains, and/or engages them.

Thanks to LinkedIn, making new connections and staying connected is easier than ever before. You can to build your "online Rolodex" throughout your career.

If your professional brand is dependent upon word-of-mouth awareness and referrals, you'll want to take a look at these statistics:

- 79% of the success from top-achieving salespeople come from relationships they have with their customers.[45]
- Prospective clients are 5x more likely to engage with a salesperson referred by a mutual acquaintance.[46]
- 44% of social buyers find vendors by looking at shared LinkedIn connections.[47]

So, how do you make new connections? Use the right etiquette. Treat your online relationships the same way you would treat your face-to-face relationships. Be personal, and let them know they matter to you.

Who can you connect with on LinkedIn? Anyone you know, and anyone you *want* to get to know. This may include:

- Past colleagues
- Current colleagues
- Former schoolmates
- Neighbours
- Other business associates
- People you've "met" or connected with on Twitter or other online groups
- People you want to get to know or who will provide value to you
- People you've been introduced to

Essentially, anyone you've crossed paths with, particularly from a business perspective.

Many people I know will not connect with their competitors on LinkedIn. They don't like to provide their competition with access to their professional network. Perhaps the industry I work in is more collaborative, but I find my "competitors" are often my best allies. Many of us share information (and even share clients when appropriate.) Whether or not you accept your competition – or any other connection – into your network is a personal choice.

MODULE #2 IS MADE UP OF THESE LESSONS:

Lesson #12: Always Be Collaborating (and Connecting.)
Lesson #13: Map Your Client's Journey Through Micro-Moments and Touchpoints.
Lesson #14: How To Make New Connections Using Social Media.
Lesson #15: Give First and Make Memorable Introductions.

LESSON #12

ALWAYS BE COLLABORATING (AND CONNECTING)

"A-B-C. A-Always, B-Be, C-Closing.
Always be closing, always be closing."
~Glengarry Glen Ross

Scratch the word *closing* and re-insert the words *collaborating* or *connecting* when it comes to social media.

Modern day sales no longer involves aggressively pushing your client into making a decision: it's about relationship-building and collaborating with them to find a solution.

Did you know 74% of prospects choose the company that was the first to help them along the buyer's journey?[48]

We love to buy, but we hate to be sold.

Gary Vaynerchuk's book *Jab, Jab, Jab, Right Hook: How To Tell Your Story In A Noisy Social World* is a great metaphor for the main point of his book, which is to "give, give, give…then ask."

Build your collateral (another C) by giving *first*, and once you've built a relationship, then you can ask your connection to take action.

By now, you've done your research about your target audience. You thoroughly understand their wants, their needs, and their fears. You've stepped into their shoes. The next step is to build rapport.

THREE STEPS TO BUILD RAPPORT ONLINE AND IN REAL LIFE (IRL)

On Wikipedia, rapport is described as:

> *"gleaning information about a problem mental state and desired goals, using specific tools and techniques to make interventions, and integrating proposed changes into the client's life. The entire process is guided by the non-verbal responses of the client.*[49]*"*

Essentially, developing good rapport is a feeling of mutual affection for one another. It can make or break a business relationship.

It's important that each touchpoint of your professional marketing builds admiration and confidence in the mind of your audience.

Whether you are sending your connection an email, calling them, or meeting face-to-face, you'll want to do your research about them in advance. Thanks to social media, you have unprecedented access to information about them. You can Google their name, look at their LinkedIn profile, or check out their presence on other social media sites.

The following are three steps you can use to develop rapport:

Step #1: Find common ground

- Do you have connections in common?
- Did you go to the same school?
- Do you have hobbies in common?

- Are they using keywords you can mirror back to them?
- What are they posting on their status updates or blog posts?
- Can you identify ways you can help them?
- When you're reaching out to make connections, use the "common ground" as an "icebreaker" (both online and IRL.)

Step #2: Be likeable

According to Dr. Robert Cialdini's six principles of influence (from his book called *Influence*), likability is very important when it comes to persuasion.

> *"We tend to like people who're similar to us, compliment us or cooperate with us in achieving mutual goals.*[50]*"*
>
> – *Dr. Robert Cialdini*

We believe people who are attractive are more likeable and trustworthy. We like people who are similar to us in interests and opinion. We also feel a sense of commonality when we collaboratively work toward a common goal.

So how does this work for *your* brand?

In real life, you can be more likeable if you smile when you're speaking. Even when you're on the phone, it affects the tone of your voice.

You can also be more likeable when you use the proper etiquette:

- Treat others the way you'd like to be treated
- Use a firm handshake
- Maintain eye contact
- Dress appropriately
- Ask open-ended questions
- Be sincere

In a nutshell, be "human."

Step #3: Mirror your connection(s)

The best way to describe mirroring: is to imitate the gesture, speech pattern, or attitude of another person. For example, if the person you're speaking to speaks quietly, you "mirror" them by also speaking quietly. Or, if the person leans in to speak, you lean in also. Mirroring helps us to develop a bond with the other person. We don't always consciously notice these behavioral patterns, but process this information on a subconscious level.

It's important to note that mirroring has to be *very* subtle, and doesn't have to be matched gesture-to-gesture. If someone crosses their arms, you cross your legs. If they lean back, wait a few moments until you also lean back. If your attempt at mirroring is too obvious, your connection may feel strange that you're copying them. (You're not a mime, or playing "Simon Says" after all.)

One way I use "mirroring" to build rapport with my clients is to learn the "language" they speak. In my pre-presentation research, I will find out if the group/audience uses the term "clients" or the word "customers". In one specific group, the audience didn't use the term "close clients;" instead, they "win assignments." When you use the specific terms and phrases your target audience uses, then you will build trust because they subconsciously recognize that you "get" them. This also works for specific acronyms used by that particular group as well. Does your audience use acronyms like CPG, NGOs, or ROI?

Be sure you thoroughly understand the terms and language your target audience uses before you try to mirror it. If you use it in the wrong context, you'll break rapport immediately and never be able to get it back.

EXERCISE #12: YOUR WEEKLY COMMITMENT TO CONNECTING AND COLLABORATING

TIME COMMITMENT: 5 MINS PER CONNECTION

I challenge you to set a weekly goal to deepen the connections within your network.

Remember to revisit your goals. What are your objectives? Who are you connected with, or who can you connect with to help you achieve these goals?

Reach out and pay it forward by messaging people in your current network each week. Commit to reaching out to at least five different people per week (that's only one connection per day!)

Ways you can reach out:

- Congratulate a connection on a new achievement.
- Comment on a blog post written by one of your connections.
- Send someone an interesting article you think they will find relevant.
- Introduce two people who could benefit from connecting with each other.
- Share one of their posts with your network on LinkedIn, Twitter (or other relevant channel.)

LESSON #13

MAP YOUR CLIENT'S JOURNEY THROUGH MICRO-MOMENTS AND TOUCHPOINTS

"The little things…there's nothing bigger, is there?"

~Vanilla Sky

According to RSR's 2014 Benchmark report, "Retail Analytics Moves to the Frontline," 49% of all respondents said their consumers expect to have instantaneous access to information about products and services everywhere.[51]

Think about a recent purchase you've made, and your experience with that brand. When you were looking for answers, or for customer service, you didn't care whether it came from the website, in-store, phone, or social media, right?

Your target audience feels the same way about your brand. They want access to answers and expect to have a seamless experience regardless of whether it's online or offline.

Yet, most of us haven't thought about providing a consistent and cohesive brand presence.

Your target audience likely uses the following decision-making process:

Stage #1: I have a problem (awareness.)

Stage #2: Who can help me with this problem? (consideration.)

- They will ask themselves: who is person/brand that is immediately top-of-mind?
- They ask their network if anyone has a resource.
- They search Google keywords or phrases.
- They will look at online reviews, articles, blogs etc.

Once they have a few options, they may narrow the decision down to three different vendors to obtain quotes and compare.

Stage #3: Purchase decision

- What does their "gut" tell them?
- What results did any of these vendors produce in the past?
- Who was the most "available" to help?

Let's take a look your presence to see if you've done a good job with developing a solid presence for inbound leads.

EXERCISE #13: MAP OUT YOUR PROSPECT'S PATH TO PURCHASE

Remember when you looked at yourself through the lens of your ideal client and that first impression? Now it's time to dive a little deeper.

Take a look at the various ways your potential client or target audience will connect with your brand.

You want to be natural go-to person who is *"top-of-mind and tip-of-tongue."*[52] (I love that quote. I read it in Jonah Berger's book *Contagious: Why Things Catch On.*)

Mapping out this framework helps you to provide the right content at the right time and gently lead prospects through the sales funnel.

You're going to want to ask yourself the following questions:

- Is your brand story easily accessible?
- Have you identified and addressed objections and problems?
- Do you listen and engage on the appropriate social media channels?
- Are you using keywords that resonate with them?
- How quickly do you respond on social media or to voicemails?

Step #1. Take an inventory of all your inbound and outbound touchpoints.

Step #2. What impact does each touchpoint have? Does it enhance or weaken their experience with your brand?

Step #3. Look at the AIDA (attention, interest, desire, action) sales funnel in Lesson #16 and develop content help to guide them on their path to purchase.

Inbound touchpoints in social media:

- LinkedIn personal page
- LinkedIn company page
- Facebook business page
- Twitter
- Instagram
- Snapchat
- Pinterest
- YouTube

Are your posts set to public or private? If your channels are set to public, is your professional brand experience consistent across all these channels?

Do you need to make your "personal network" posts or photos private so that it doesn't conflict with your professional brand?

INBOUND TOUCHPOINTS ON YOUR WEBSITE/BLOG

- Do you have a lead magnet to obtain email addresses?
- What are your site stats?
- Have you featured testimonials or online reviews?

OUTBOUND TOUCHPOINTS: FACE-TO-FACE OR VIA PHONE

- How do you appear at a conference or other event?
- What is the experience like when being introduced through a mutual connection?
- Do you respond promptly?
- How do you engage with a word-of-mouth referral?

OTHER TOUCHPOINTS:

- Press
- Advertising
- Packaging
- Demos

Every micro-moment and touchpoint can enhance or diminish your brand.

Remember: You don't need to be everywhere. You only need to be where your target audience is.

I suggest you focus on "owning" one channel at a time. As you become more comfortable, you can move onto other channels. Since LinkedIn is the professional network, I'd recommend you start there.

Now it's your turn, map out at least five touchpoints your target audience will have with your brand. Is their experience consistent with the image you want to portray of yourself? What strategies can you put into place to make the experience even better?

TIME COMMITMENT: 10 MINUTES PER TOUCHPOINT.

Touchpoint #1:

_____

_____

Strategy to make the experience better:

_____

_____

Touchpoint #2.

_____

_____

Strategy to make the experience better:

_____

_____

Touchpoint #3.

_____

_____

Strategy to make the experience better:

_____

Touchpoint #4.

_____

_____

Strategy to make the experience better:

_____

Touchpoint #5.

_____

_____

Strategy to make the experience better:

_____

_____

_____

_____

_____

_____

_____

_____

_____

_____

DEEP THOUGHTS ABOUT MAKING CONNECTIONS WITH YOUR BRAND

There are multiple different approaches to building your brand and making quality connections using LinkedIn, Twitter, and other social media channels.

As my cousin Jim Kenny says, "when you plant corn, you get corn" (otherwise referred to in the Bible as "for whatsoever a man sows, that shall he also reap.")

When we come from a place of abundance, when we give first and pay-it-forward, and when we come from a place of service, people (and money) will naturally gravitate towards you.

Etiquette matters. We may be connecting computer-to-computer, but we are fundamentally connecting human-to-human. The Golden Rule of "do unto others" still holds true online.

Entrepreneur, author and leadership speaker, Jim Rohn said:

"The challenge of leadership is to be strong, but not rude; be kind but not weak; be bold, but not bully; be thoughtful, but not lazy; be humble, but not timid; be proud, but not arrogant; have humor, but without folly."

That just about sums it all up, doesn't it?

LESSON #14

MAKE NEW CONNECTIONS USING SOCIAL MEDIA

"Your network is your net worth."

~Tim Sanders

We don't exchange business cards without a conversation, and this applies to online (n)etiquette on LinkedIn as well.

I always do my best to send a personalized connection request by reminding my connection how we met, or why I'd like to get to know them.

You can also leverage LinkedIn's three degrees of separation, to see who can introduce you to your dream client or dream connection.

THE 3-STEP PROCESS TO CONNECT WITH YOUR DREAM CLIENT/CONNECTION USING LINKEDIN:

Step #1: SEARCH: for your dream connection/ideal client on LinkedIn.

Using the search field or the advanced link, you can search for the person or company you would like to connect with.

Step #2: SEEK: Research their profile to see if you can find ways to build commonalities and break the ice with non-business conversation.

LinkedIn states that the average user has 930 connections.[53] As of June 2016, the LinkedIn network at large has over 450 million members in over 200 countries[54]. Your potential reach is exponential!

Step #3: ASK: Introduce yourself directly to your "dream connection," or ask someone in your network to introduce you (whenever possible).

According to LinkedIn, "prospects are 5x more likely to engage with a salesperson referred by a mutual acquaintance.[55]" And, 44% of buyers find potential vendors by looking at shared LinkedIn connections, according to IDC.[56]

(Note: This is again, why *quality* connections are important. You would never ask a loose connection to do you a favor. Be mindful that most people have added connections without really knowing them first.)

HOW I USED THIS THREE-STEP PROCESS TO OBTAIN A NEW OPPORTUNITY

I used this three-step process to get introduced to the Associate Dean at the Faculty of Business and IT at the University of Ontario Institute of Technology (UOIT). I asked my first degree connection to introduce me to the Associate Dean. I reached out to him via LinkedIn, obtained a meeting, and within a few months I was hired as an Instructor for the Social Media Marketing Certificate program at the Management Development Centre (MDC).

If you've already got a strong brand online, and you're able to obtain an introduction from a mutual acquaintance, you've got a good start at converting their business!

OR, YOU CAN JUST REACH OUT AND CONNECT

If you don't have a mutual connection, you can simply reach out and introduce yourself. Never sell from the start. I recommend going with a personalized connection request "icebreaker" such as:

> "Hi Sam, I noticed you are a part of the XYZ Group on LinkedIn and I think we may have a lot in common when it comes to the _____ industry. I'd like to learn more about what your business does. I'd love to connect with you here on LinkedIn."

or

> "Hi Chris, I noticed on your LinkedIn profile that you enjoy golfing. I have a membership at ABC Golf Club. I'd love to get to know your business better and would be happy to take you out on the links! In the meantime, I'd like to stay connected with you here on LinkedIn."

One of the clients I was working with mentioned that he was using LinkedIn to reach out to other "circles of influence" within his 1st degree connections. He would simply look at the high-level connections of his 1st degree connections with and reach out to say:

> "Hi Dave, I noticed we are both connected to Linda Anderson. Linda has been a client and friend of mine for a number of years. I'd love to connect with you here on LinkedIn."

He didn't pitch from the get-go, but he followed up and nurtured the relationship with various gentle reminders using social media.

This, my friends, is what's called "Social Selling."

CONNECT WITH DREAM CLIENTS USING LINKEDIN GROUPS

I know that some LinkedIn Groups can be very valuable for specific niches.

You can reach out to various potential connections using LinkedIn Groups by:

- Answering questions
- Asking questions
- Joining conversations

Using your Ideal Client Avatar exercise, look for potential groups your target audience uses online. Are they engaging in conversations here? Provide value as often as you can.

HOW TO CONNECT WITH MULTIPLE DECISION-MAKERS

If you actively sell, or if there are multiple decision-makers involved in the process to hire you, or buy your products/services, it's wise to cover all your bases by reaching out and connecting with several people within the organization. Connecting with multiple stakeholders can help you to gain influence when it comes to the decision-making process.

LinkedIn recommends this "multi-threading" approach because their data shows that firms deal with on average at least four individuals to close a sale.[57]

It's a good backup if your first point of contact has moved to a different department or obtains a new opportunity at a different company.

When it comes to an important decision within a big company, find ways to connect with multiple stakeholders.

HOW TO REPLY TO CONNECTION REQUESTS FROM STRANGERS USING LINKEDIN

I'm sure you've received a mountain of connection requests from strangers. You may wonder: *"who is this person, and what do they want from me?"*

I receive requests from strangers every day, but I firmly believe that I want to build my network based on valuable connections. They have to find value in my connection and vice versa.

I'm open to meeting new people. I also want to be sure I have a conversation with a stranger before I accept their request.

You can reply to requests from strangers in one of two ways:

Option #1. Reply to the connection request by clicking on the "reply" button whenever you receive the notification from LinkedIn via email.

> *"Thank you (name) for invitation to connect. Can you please refresh my memory as to how we know each other?"*

This way, you put the ball back in their court to qualify why they want to connect with you. If they don't reply, you don't accept their request because you wouldn't want this person in your online Rolodex anyway.

Option #2. Accept the connection request and reply on LinkedIn's messaging platform with a request to meet or chat on the phone:

> *"Thank you for the invitation to connect (name.) I don't think we've met before but I'd like to get to know your business better. I'd love to get together with you for a coffee and chat about how we might be able to help each other."*

I have only used Option #2 on a couple of occasions. A well-recognized award-winning entrepreneur in Toronto, Jody Steinhauer, sent me a generic connection request. I replied with the copy above and expected to only spend about five minutes with her.

Instead of a five-minute meeting, we spent an hour and a half chatting. At the end of the time we spent together, she graciously and generously said "I'd love to help you with your business. Is there anyone in my network I can introduce you to?"

That one simple tactic, turned a standard connection request into a meeting, and which opened up my opportunity to make new, high-level connections.

Face-to-face meetings are time consuming, but you can see how valuable this time spent was for me! I can now reach out to this connection at any time to ask her for an introduction to her network.

HOW TO CONNECT WITH PROSPECTS USING TWITTER

Let me start by saying, you don't have to use Twitter. This channel has changed a lot in the past few years. In 2010, Twitter was a *very* valuable hub where I connected with a lot of Canadian bloggers and influencers. Eventually, many of us who had "met" on Twitter were connecting in real life at blogging conferences such as ShesConnected and Blissdom Canada. Instead of walking into a room full of strangers, we already were "friends" with most of the attendees simply because we had connected on Twitter first.

In the past few years, I've found Twitter to be more of a news-based platform with pushed content, instead of a place to engage in conversations.

However, if your target audience or dream client is actively using Twitter, you can use this channel to engage with them:

Get to know their likes and interests by following their tweets (you can learn what they are interested in both personally and professionally). Jump into conversations that aren't necessarily business-related.

If they ask questions such as: "Does anyone know the best burger joint downtown?" Reply to the tweet and mention your favorite spot.

On Twitter, because it's a public forum, comments from strangers are expected.

These same principles about open communication often apply to other social media sites as well (Instagram, Snapchat, blogs etc.) As long as the person's posts are set to public, they know their posts are being shared with a large network, so it's an open invitation to join a conversation, as long as it's relevant.

EXERCISE #14: REACH OUT AND MAKE NEW CONNECTIONS

TIME COMMITMENT: 5 MINS PER NEW CONNECTION

Each week, set a plan in place with a goal of how many new connections you are going to make. Think about the objectives of your professional brand and set your targets based on what you hope to achieve.

Each week, I will reach out to connect with _____ new people.

Let's say you reach out to 10 new connections each week and you work 47 weeks per year. That's 470 new connections each year.

How many of those new connections turn into clients? _____

How much is each new client worth? _____

Starting to see the value of making those new connections?

LESSON #15

GIVE FIRST AND MAKE MEMORABLE INTRODUCTIONS

"The heart that gives, gathers."

~Tao Te Ching

As we've discussed, one of the easiest ways to build collateral with your connections to "give value first" is through mutual introductions.

A few years ago, a financial advisor Terry Aldred reached out to me via LinkedIn. It was a "cold introduction," meaning he didn't ask anyone to introduce us, but he did send a personalized connection request to introduce himself.

Terry followed up with me via LinkedIn to book a meeting over coffee, and while I was reluctant to meet, he gently persisted just to say *"I'd just like to get to know your business better."* (As a small business owner who was looking to grow my client base, anyone who could help spread word-of-mouth about my business made for a valuable meeting.)

Instead of directly pitching me about his services, Terry steered the conversation to ask me about my business. After I gave him the run-down of what I do, Terry offered to introduce me to people in his network who could benefit from my training and services.

Within the week, Terry delivered upon is promise. He reached out to at least three different connections with introductions similar to:

> *"Hi Roger, I just met with Leslie Hughes from PUNCH!media this week. Leslie specializes in LinkedIn training and profile writing. I think you both may find this connection to be useful and I'll leave it to Leslie to introduce herself when she has a moment."*

Terry copied me on the correspondence and the ball was left in my court to take the next step. Terry's approach of giving first, got him a new client because he didn't *sell*, he *helped*.

So guess who's got two thumbs and hired Terry as my advisor? This gal!

THE WORLD'S BEST INTRODUCTION

I want to share with you the very best mutual introduction I have ever received. This intro was made by a client of mine, Nate Isaacson. When he would make an introduction to a mutual connection, he would send copy that read similar to:

> *"Hi Leslie,*
>
> *I wanted to introduce you to Paul, who is the Financial Advisor for ABC Company. A few things that you should know about Paul: he is originally from a small town in Georgia and is a huge fan of punk music. He is married and has one child.*
>
> *Paul - As I mentioned earlier today, I would like to introduce you to Leslie Hughes <https://ca.linkedin.com/in/leslielhughes>, the founder of PUNCH!Media. She is based up in Toronto, and has worked with several of the executives at Guardian including Susan, Matt and Erin to help them optimize their LinkedIn profiles. Leslie is one of two people I've met who has visited Cuba. She is super easy to work with and recently*

was featured on CTV's "The Social" as an expert on the importance of maximizing your digital presence (https://youtu.be/Vee-48IA-Ms).

Here is what you can expect in working with her. Leslie will work with you and/or your assistant to schedule a one-hour phone interview where she will ask you a bunch of questions to get to know you and to learn about your business. She will then take your responses and create a professional tagline, your summary, and your current experience along with a few other areas of your profile. You will have as many back-and-forths as you need to get the profile to where you like it and can get it approved by Compliance.

I'll leave it to Leslie to follow up and book a time with you."

What I love about this introduction is that he familiarizes the people he is introducing—not only with the role of each person—but he will often add in some miscellaneous personal trivia that is both interesting and helps to break the ice. These random facts are both unexpected and delightful.

EXERCISE #15: PAY-IT-FORWARD BY INTRODUCING NEW CONNECTIONS EACH WEEK.

TIME COMMITMENT: 2 MINUTES PER INTRODUCTION

Whether you do this through LinkedIn or via email, commit to introducing at least two people who could mutually benefit from an introduction.

Your pay-it-forward generosity will make a great impression and people will remember to reciprocate when they time is right.

Make it a commitment: Each week, I will reach out to introduce _____ new people.

MODULE #3

CONVERT

Sales gets a bad rap, doesn't it?

What are some of the images or people who come to mind when I say "sales" or "salesman?"

You may think of words such as:

- Hustler
- Liar
- Con-artist
- Greedy
- Slimy
- Aggressive

For me, a stereotypical salesman comes in the form of Herb Tarlek from the TV show *WKRP in Cincinnati*. With his matching white shoes and white belt, oozing and schmoozing, Herb would do anything to convert a client.

Unlike Herb, who was smarmy, when I was working in advertising sales, my first priority was to always be sincere and ensure that my clients' needs came first, no matter how much or how little money they invested. I actually considered myself to be a horrible salesperson because I never liked to "close the sale." Instead, I was focused on providing value.

Our target market's access to information via Google allows them to be much more educated, and more skeptical, than ever before. So our "secret sauce," or intellectual capital, isn't as important as it used to be. Instead, we are now collaborators with our target market. We no longer *tell* them the solution, we work *with* them to produce results.

You may not think you're in sales, but as a brand, you are selling yourself. Daniel Pink points out in his book *To Sell Is Human*[58], "we're all in sales now and the denomination is time, attention, effort, energy, commitment, etc."

THE ROLE OF SOCIAL SELLING

"Social Selling" is a new buzz term to explain how we can use social media to research and connect with our target market.

PeopleLinx's State of Social Selling Report[59] found that while 76% of business-to-business (B2B) sales reps recognize the value, only 24% of B2B sales professionals feel they *know* how to use social media for selling.

Yet, when companies offer social sales training to their teams, the number of reps who *say* they use social networks as part of their sales process jumps from 28% to 74%. (Hmmmm. I wonder.)

Did you know:

- 81% of buyers are more likely to engage when their company is well-known and has a strong professional brand?[60]
- 86% of buyers will listen if sales professionals provide insights about their business?[61]
- 77% of buyers are more likely to choose a vendor if the salesperson is informed about their business needs?[62]
- 69% of buyers are more likely to choose a vendor if the salesperson is recommended to them by someone in their professional network?[63]

Sales and your brand go hand in hand. (I'm a poet and I didn't even know it!)

MODULE #3 IS MADE UP OF THESE LESSONS:

Lesson #16: The Old Sales Funnel Vs The New Sales Funnel.
Lesson #17: How To Sell When You Hate Selling.
Lesson #18: Teach Them Something New.
Lesson #19: Define The Sales Triggers and Ways You Can Reach Out.
Lesson #20: Designing Seductive Inbound Lead Magnets.
Lesson #21: Infomercials and The Persuasive "Science" Behind How They Get Their Target Audience to Buy.
Lesson #22: How to Overcome Sales Objections and Close The Deal.
Lesson #23: After The Sale is Where The Fun Begins.
Lesson #24: Referrals: The Next Generation.
Lesson #25: Influencers and Viral Marketing

"Everyone lives by selling something."

- Robert Louis Stevenson

How do you feel when you see your target audience or client's eyes light up because you've provided them with a solution to their problem?

Even though I use the word "convert" throughout this book (because it works with the alliteration,) I don't feel that I sell. Instead, I believe I empower people to make decisions with the proper insights and education.

I absolutely thrive when I see my audience nodding their head or putting pen to paper because I've triggered a new insight for them.

Now that we've covered your brand, and we've made strides to build and deepen relationships, this last section focuses on building thought leadership and using a holistic approach to your strategy. This means that we are looking at constructing your brand from the "big picture" and narrowing down all the action items to make it happen.

Remember, "Rome wasn't built in a day" so dominating your niche is going to take some time and some "hustle." Be sure to stay focused on your goals and commit to a plan of action. Every step you're taking forward on your journey to success will be worth it.

Recognize that you are bringing your unique gifts to the world. Your target audience needs you, so "stay the course" and reap the rewards.

HOLISTIC STRATEGY: OWNED, EARNED, AND PAID

I realize that social media is overwhelming. This is what I focus on *all* day, *every* day, and I'm overwhelmed by staying on top of it all.

Combining a marketing mix of "owned," "earned," and "paid" content is a holistic and strategic way to extend your brand awareness.

OWNED MEDIA: CONTENT THAT *YOU* OWN

As we discussed in Chapter #1, you are your media agency. You have complete control over the content you share with your audience. This "owned" media includes keyword-rich content for your blog (so you rank higher in SEO) and your newsletter.

I typically tell my clients to do their best to "own" the relationship with their target audience by building their email database and sending out an e-newsletter.

Capturing email addresses is important for your brand because you want to be able to maintain contact with your target audience. Social media sites constantly change. Some sites change their algorithm or today's "hot" channel can become yesterday's news.

Social media channels have been called "walled gardens" because they own their network along with when and if their members actually see your content. Your audience also has to be a member of these social media sites to access the information.

Owning your content by publishing a blog and/or a newsletter is a much better way to ensure your audience sees your messages.

(Also, when you "own" the email addresses, you can find ways to reach out and connect with your audience across multiple different social media channels. For example, you can upload this email database to each site to find your followers and engage with them there!)

EARNED MEDIA: CONTENT THAT YOUR USERS SHARE

Earned content is attention you "earn" through word-of-mouth awareness.

This is when someone clicks "Like" on your content, comments on your post, and/or shares it with their network. As we've already discussed, this third-party endorsement is usually trusted and credible, and can be a great way to generate awareness to a whole new audience.

PAID MEDIA: CONTENT YOU PAY TO DISTRIBUTE (otherwise known as Advertising)

As more and more people are turning to the Internet for news and information, we are seeing a huge shift of revenue from traditional advertising to digital platforms.

If my clients are interested in advertising, I usually recommend they look at "native advertising," or non-interruptive based advertising, because these ads appear to be more effective at getting attention on social media channels[64]. Not only are people blocking "pop ups," but many of us have also become "blind" to seeing display ads.

We haven't covered a lot of Facebook in this book, but as a channel for advertising, Facebook certainly is worth considering. You can do a deep dive with psychographic targeting, you can pay only when someone meets the objectives you've outlined, and Facebook advertising is quite affordable for even the smallest of budgets. If you are investing with ads on Facebook, the "Dark Posts" used through Power Editor on Chrome are one of the most effective ways to reach your audience (but this process is fairly complicated and time consuming.)

From my experience, advertising on LinkedIn is more expensive than Facebook ads, and (as of today) is suitable only if you want to target by demographic. Since LinkedIn is my "channel of choice," and the social media site where my target audience invests their time, I've purchased sponsored posts to reach a specific audience. I found it to be an interesting exercise and I plan to re-visit sponsoring a post in the future.

In addition to Facebook and LinkedIn, there are plenty of other forms of online advertising, including banner ads, search ads on Google, Twitter "cards," YouTube ads, and more.

Before you begin investing in advertising, you'll want to circle back to the Ideal Client Avatar exercise and critically assess why and how you will use this tactic on the channel(s) that your target audience uses.

Each aspect of the "owned," "earned," and "paid" approach can be effective on its own, but combined together is a one, two, three punch!

LESSON #16

THE OLD SALES FUNNEL VS THE NEW SALES FUNNEL

"Show me the money!"

~Jerry Maguire

A sales funnel is pretty self explanatory: it's a process your clients will go through on their path to purchase (or path to persuade.)

Many different sales funnels have been created and defined over the years. The following are just a few basic, common approaches.

Like the discussion we just had about a holistic owned, earned, and paid approach, I believe you need to use *both* the "old" model and the "new" model for optimum success. It's important to cast a wide net to get new clients into your sales funnel, and it's also useful to laser-focus on personalizing your message and courting ideal clients long before they are even aware they need you.

SALES FUNNEL #1: THE "OLD" SALES FUNNEL

A common traditional sales funnel is known by the acronym AIDA, which stands for:

- Awareness
- Interest
- Desire
- Action

AWARENESS

The goal of awareness in the sales funnel is to cast a wide net and draw attention to your brand.

In a traditional sales funnel, brands use a "spray and pray" method where they focus their content on advertising (print, radio, TV, online, etc.) and "pray" that their target audience will see their message and buy their stuff. (Paid media.)

The "sweet spot" to build awareness through advertising is a combination of both *reach* and *frequency*.

Reach: the number of people that had been exposed to the medium (TV, newspapers, magazines etc.)

Frequency: the number of times viewers were exposed to the same brand or ad.

Advertising needs repeated to the target audience because one ad rarely converts new business. Frequency helps to familiarize the target audience with your brand and helps to build trust.

Through social media marketing, you can generate brand awareness through disseminating your content. As I mentioned, you are a media agency, so when your brand publishes relevant copy and/or videos through blogging, you have an opportunity to reach your audience through current followers, and perhaps if Google ranks your post high in their ranking (via SEO). (Owned media.)

You will also generate awareness for your brand when your followers engage with your posts and *their* connections see your content. This is typically one of the most trustworthy ways of earning attention. (Earned media.)

Here's how you can generate awareness for your brand using social media:

- Post blogs on your site and long form blog posts on LinkedIn to build thought leadership. At the end of the blog post, always be sure to include a short description about who you are and how people can reach you (in case it's the first point of contact.)
- Make sure your LinkedIn Summary is well-written and is fascinating to your target audience. People may search for you based on keywords, or may be referred by a mutual connection.
- Reach out and make new, relevant connections on LinkedIn.
- Include a snippet of your blog post in your newsletter and tease the reader to click through to read more.
- Engage on other people's social media channels by commenting and/or sharing their status updates or posts. Focus on your objectives: who are your hot prospects and/or dream connections? Engage with them and promote them to your network.
- Join relevant groups where your prospects may be engaging on LinkedIn and jump into conversations with them.
- Follow and engage with your target audience on other social

media channels such as Twitter or Instagram.

- Find influencers or brand ambassadors who can help you share your message.
- Consider investing in advertising on channel(s) where your target audience spends their time. In my opinion, non-interruptive "native advertising" works better than standard ads.
- Native advertising is where the ad is non-interruptive. It's usually seen in the feed of the social media site, acknowledged by a small font saying "sponsored" or "promoted," On LinkedIn, "native advertising" comes in the form of a promoted blog post. On Facebook, it can be a boosted post, or a "Dark Post" which is best managed through Facebook's Power Editor on a Chrome browser.

INTEREST

Once you've captured the attention from your target audience, the next step is to build interest.

Your messages should be designed to pique their curiosity so your target audience leans in further to find out more about your brand.

Using social media, how can you tell when your target audience is interested in your brand?

- They subscribe to your newsletter and/or follow you on your social media channels.
- They reach out directly and ask you a question via email or other channel.
- They engage with your online content. They look at your LinkedIn profile.
- They download a "whitepaper" or other lead magnet and provide their email for valuable content (we'll talk about lead magnets in Lesson #20)

To pique your target audience's interest, you want to create a hook that draws them in. Building your email database is one of the most powerful ways you can "own" your relationship. The best way is to give them something of value in exchange.

Give your audience something for free, and then continue to build trust through a newsletter.

Here are some ways you can generate interest using social media:

- Deliver relevant copy that educates, entertains, or engages your target audience. This may include blog posts, webinars, "free reports," live question and answer sessions.
- Be "human". People prefer to connect with a person instead of a logo.
- Ensure you have a dynamic image and/or video that complements the copy.
- Develop a passionate community within your social media network. When they engage, others will lean in to find out more too.
- Whenever possible, include a call-to-action to capture their email address. Or, be sure to include "boilerplate" copy with your unique value proposition along with a way for people to reach you, such as your email address or website URL.
- Do your best to draw them in with specific language such as "click here" or "sign up now." People won't intuitively know to do this unless you tell them.

DESIRE

It's exciting when you take your audience's interest to a new level. Creating desire for your brand moves their interest from a "want-to-have" to a "must-have." Your target audience is in a "consideration phase" and are moving closer to purchase. Now is the time to really highlight the benefits and value of your brand and your core offer or idea. Address any objections and include a call-to-action for next steps to solidify the transaction.

Some of the ways you can tell if your target audience has desire when using social media:

- They ask for a demonstration or a quote for services.
- They ask questions or engage with you further.

ACTION

Action is fairly straightforward. It's when someone does something. Ideally you want them to take action and/or pay for a retainer, deposit or complete the contract.

This path to purchase (or path to persuasion) isn't always linear. The prospect can bounce back between interest and desire a few times, and take multiple approaches before they make a decision.

Remember: you may think the process ends with the sale, when actually the process is just *beginning* for your client. Be sure to over-deliver with a lot of follow up to ensure they are happy with the process.

With delivering an "over the top" experience, you'll be able to obtain testimonials, referrals, and perhaps even "upsell" in the future. (We will be talking more about referrals and generating word-of-mouth awareness in Lesson #25)

SALES FUNNEL #2: THE "NEW" SALES FUNNEL

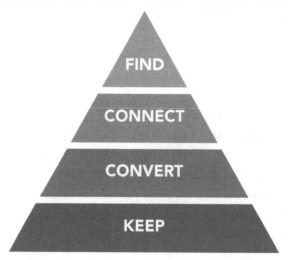

In the "new" sales funnel, the path to purchase is inverted. Instead of *pushing* out to your network, you *pull* them in. This is where the Ideal Client Avatar really comes in handy!

Social media has allowed us to learn so much more about our target audience. The amount of information your target audience publishes about themselves is staggering.

From a personal perspective, it's creepy to be followed and documented by the companies who are tracking the information we publish about ourselves. But from marketing perspective, all this information is *golden*.

Brands no longer have to guess where their target audience is, and what they want, we can see where they are by looking, listening and gathering data. Since most of the social media sites' default is set to "public", it's easy to do a deep dive and research your target audience.

While the "old" sales funnel is wide at the top and narrows on the way down, the "new" sales funnel is inverted: it's narrow at the top and widens at the bottom.

The steps through the "new" sales funnel are as follows:

- Find
- Connect
- Convert
- Keep

FIND

Using social media, you can research your audience's wants and needs by finding them on the channel(s) they use most. Essentially you "fish where the fish are." On LinkedIn, you can simply search by company, industry and/or by title to gather as much information as possible.

Or, perhaps your target audience "finds" you. They may see one of your blog posts when researching keywords or phrases on Google, or perhaps someone referred you to a prospect.

CONNECT

Making one-on-one connections and/or getting face-to-face meetings are always more meaningful than having a brand send generic messages.

You can use social media to connect to your target audience by:

- Having someone introduce you to a quality connection on LinkedIn.
- Reach out and send a personalized connection request.
- Joining niche groups online (Facebook, LinkedIn etc.) and participate in online conversations.
- Following people from your target audience on Twitter and engage in conversations.
- "Liking," commenting, or sharing their posts.

(There's more where this came from Lesson #13)

CONVERT

Quite simply, "convert" is the same step as "ACTION" in the "old" sales funnel.

KEEP

For many organizations, "keeping" your target audience happy is one of the most often overlooked, but most powerful strategies. A former boss of mine always used to say, "*a bird in the hand is worth two in the bush.*" It's much more economical to keep your current clients happy, and keep them in your sales funnel than to consistently focus on obtaining new clients.

And yet, I see many companies who focus almost exclusively on acquisition. They don't realize that the sales relationship actually *begins* when the transaction happens.

Some unique ways to keep your current clients happy:

- Engage with them on social media. It's simple, cost-efficient, and effective!
- Offer them a discount to another vendor's services.
- Random acts of kindness: provide them with free access to a low-cost product or service.
- Upgrade their status (move from member to VIP.)
- Send a handwritten thank you card.
- Offer free shipping for products.
- Invite them to an event or exclusive webinar.
- Send them a "Happy Work Anniversary" message.
- Send cards during a made-up or unusual holiday "Happy Groundhog Day!"

Most importantly, make your target audience feel important and special.

EXERCISE #16: CONVERSION TACTICS

TIME COMMITMENT: 2+ HOURS

Identify five conversion tactics you can use to guide your target audience through the sales funnel (old and/or new) and these align these strategies with an action plan.

PART OF THE SALES FUNNEL/CONVERSION TACTIC	WHAT ACTION YOU WILL TAKE	HOW HAVE YOU ASKED YOUR PROSPECT TO TAKE ACTION?
1.		
2.		
3.		
4.		
5.		

LESSON #17

HOW TO SELL WHEN YOU HATE SELLING

"To sell well is to convince someone else to part with resources – not to deprive that person, but to leave him better off in the end."

~Daniel Pink

If the thought of selling leaves you feeling "icky," there are various ways you can reframe your perspective so that sales feels less slimy or pushy.

You aren't selling, you're *helping* your prospects. They have a problem; you have a solution. It's a win-win! Your target audience *needs* you. They need your insights and expertise. In fact, you are actually *hurting* your prospects when you hold back, because they will miss out on all the great information you know about. Your client will perceive your products/services have more value when you stand in your value and charge what you are worth. Feel congruent with your value, and you'll find your products, services or ideas will almost sell themselves!

When I was researching the quote "money goes where the attention flows," I came across these seven fundamental principles of the Hawaiian Huna tradition:

IKE – The world is what you think it is.
KALA – There are no limits, everything is possible.
MAKIA – Energy flows where attention goes.
MANAWA – Now is the moment of power.
ALOHA – To love is to be happy with.
MANA – All power comes from within.
PONO – Effectiveness is the measure of truth.

Think about selling, acquiring attention and making money from a positive perspective. Money is abundant and plentiful. Get in the right mindset that you are providing *value* and that value is worth being compensated for.

EXERCISE #17: WRITE DOWN AT LEAST ONE WAY YOU CAN REFRAME ANY NEGATIVE FEELINGS YOU HAVE ABOUT SELLING

TIME COMMITMENT: 5 MINUTES.

LESSON #18

SALES TRIGGERS, INFLUENCE AND WAYS YOU CAN REACH OUT

"I skate to where the puck is going to be, not where it has been."

~Wayne Gretzky

Being one step ahead of your target audience is a great way to build trust with your prospects. Social media is a wonderland of subtle cues, or "tells," that can help you identify when your prospect is ready to receive your help.

"Tells" are used in poker terminology. They are changes in a player's behavior or demeanor that can often indicate to the other players at the table if the player has a good hand or a bad one.

"Tells" can also be identified as sales triggers. Once you see the sales trigger, you can gently reach out, provide opportunities and deepen relationships – all from behind your computer.

According to LinkedIn, sales reps who respond quickly to trigger events via social media saw a 9.5% increase in annual revenue.[65]

Some top sales triggers:

TRIGGER	WHERE YOU MAY SEE THE TRIGGER
Change of job	LinkedIn notification/announcement
Asking questions to their network	Friend/family on social media (Facebook, Twitter), questions on LinkedIn etc.
New customer announcement	LinkedIn, company newsletter, press releases
Company relocation or expansion	Announcement on website, company newsletter, press releases
New product/service launch	Social media, newsletter
Dissatisfaction with current vendor	Industry news, social media
New legislation	News
Awards	Social media, announcement on website, company newsletter, press releases

What's important to note is that you should have already built a relationship with the prospect prior to acting on these announcements. This way, you can nurture the lead instead of trying to accelerate and force the sales process.

SALES TRIGGERS AND INFLUENCE

There's a common saying: *"People love to buy, but they hate to feel like they've been sold to."*

One of the best books I've read about Social Psychology is *Influence: The Psychology of Persuasion* by Dr. Robert Cialdini. In this book, and his TED Talk, he outlines six ways to get people to say "YES."

These six principles are:

- Reciprocity
- Commitment & Consistency
- Liking
- Authority
- Social Proof
- Scarcity

PRINCIPLE #1: RECIPROCITY

Have you ever noticed when you get something for free, you'll often feel compelled to reciprocate?

I don't know if you had them in your city, but when I think about the principle of reciprocity, I think about the "squeegee kids" who would stand at an underpass or corner and offer to clean your windshield. Even when you said *no*, and they still forcibly cleaned your windshield. I'd often feel compelled to give them a dollar for their work even when I didn't want them to clean the windshield in the first place!

Or, when I'm shopping at Costco and someone is handing out free samples, I feel obligated to buy the item just to please the person who handing them out.

How to use "reciprocity" using social media:

- On your website, include a strong lead magnet where you provide your audience with valuable information in exchange for obtaining their email address. (See Lesson #20 for more information about lead magnets.)

- LinkedIn testimonials: If you *give* a testimonial to someone you'd stake your professional reputation on, LinkedIn will prompt the person to write a testimonial in return.
- Providing advice via your blog, newsletter etc., can subtly build reciprocity because you're giving away information for free.

PRINCIPLE #2: COMMITMENT AND CONSISTENCY

When people commit orally or in writing, they are more likely to stick with it. We like to honor our work and we don't like to back out of "deals." If you ask people to make a small commitment, or encourage them to take your product for a "test drive," you'll be more likely to get them to commit.

I noticed how this principle worked when I was on vacation. My son and I went to a bicycle rental shop and salesperson went out of their way to find the right bike for my son to try out. That small commitment of getting my son to get on the bike, and then making sure he felt comfortable with the size, solidified the sale that we would rent it for the week. I noticed that once my son said "yes" to the size of the bike, it was a natural "yes" to close the sale. (The principle of reciprocity could also be applied here. The salesperson was doing something nice for us, and I felt obligated to purchase.)

How to use "commitment and consistency" using social media:

- When prospects download material from a landing page, or sign up to your newsletter, include copy that says "*Yes! I'd like to receive this information.*" Once they have subscribed, people are less likely to unsubscribe.
- Build the relationship slowly through small commitments and then build financial commitments over time. If they agree to exchange their email for free content (and they find the free

content has great value,) then when you ask them to commit to a nominal fee for the next item, they might be more likely to say yes.

- As you build trust and increase the value you provide, you can also increase the price point as you deepen your relationship.

PRINCIPLE #3: LIKING

If your prospect likes you, or feels a kinship, they are likely to buy from you. (This is where your Ideal Client Avatar exercise really comes in handy!) Or, if someone finds you attractive, they are more likely to want to work with you.

Some of the ways you can build liking is through your physical attractiveness, giving compliments, cooperating towards a common goal, and finding similarities in terms of interests, personality and background.

How to use "liking" using social media:

- Use images of your (smiling) face on your marketing material. Be sure to include your face as your avatar on various social media channels: people are less likely to want to engage with a logo.
- Show that you're a human. Write "friendly" copy. People prefer to read copy that sounds like the way we speak in real life. Avoid complicated language. Mirror or mimic words that your target audience is familiar with.

Some social media widgets (i.e. Facebook) will allow you to include buttons that show faces of "friends who like this page." The subconscious trigger is that if their friends like your page or profile, maybe they will too!

Obtain LinkedIn testimonials from people who fit your "Ideal Client Avatar". This way, prospects who fit the mould will think, "*if Sally who is just like me, likes and trusts this person, maybe I will too.*"

Acknowledge in your LinkedIn Summary or Current Position that you understand the specific challenges and frustrations of their industry. They'll feel like you truly understand their situation and know how to solve their problem.

PRINCIPLE #4: AUTHORITY

We trust experts and authority. People in these roles can have advanced education, or rank higher in terms of position at an organization (i.e. Executive level). People in authority can be doctors, lawyers, C-suite executives, or anyone who has been successful in their career.

How to use "authority" using social media:

- Highlight your education and credentials on your LinkedIn profile.
- Cite awards you've received and/or any accolades your company has received.
- Indicate if you've done public speaking and/or if you've had articles published for you, or about you.
- Obtain testimonials to highlight your expertise (this is particularly effective when the person who is giving the testimonial is well-recognized and respected within the niche of your target audience as well.)

PRINCIPLE #5: SOCIAL PROOF

We've talked about "Social Proof" quite a bit already. We look to others feedback and trust their reviews, testimonials and recommendations. Third party endorsements go much further than self-promotion.

How to use "social proof" using social media:

- Include case studies of happy clients in your blog or other social media posts.

- Testimonials on LinkedIn are terrific "social proof."
- Ask your clients to provide a review of your services on other sites like Yelp or Google.
- If you've been featured on TV or well-recognized sites, include "As seen on____."

Sometimes a subscriber count, or social shares can make you appear as if you are an influencer (but be careful of "vanity metrics".)

PRINCIPLE #6: SCARCITY

Nobody wants to miss out. Whether it's actual or perceived, the feeling we lose out on an opportunity is *very* compelling. This FOMO (fear of missing out) resides in our amygdala, and can make your prospects feel anxious if they don't take action now.

One of the most interesting examples of scarcity I've seen is through the retailer Lululemon. Have you ever noticed, this retailer became *very* popular without spending any money on media advertising?

I read an article in Canadian Business that states they use scarcity as a strategy[66]. By limiting the number of items in the same stock, customers feel compelled to buy expensive items because there is "only one left in your size."

How to use "scarcity" using social media:

- Let your audience know there is only limited availability (short-term trials). i.e. "Only X left!"
- Identify that popular products are "out of stock" or "not currently available" and encourage them to join the mailing list now so they can be first in line for the new release.
- Add time-limited tactics with countdown timers. If access to the content or products is only available for a certain amount of time, they will be more likely to take action. I.e. "Today only!"

Now, let's take a look at some other powerful sales strategies:

PRICING STRATEGY

A business' goal is to maximize sales and increase profits. Pricing is often based on a series of factors. Which of the following is *your* model?

Pricing Model #1: Premium Pricing

Like Tiffany, you can charge more because you're best in class, unique or a specialty item or service.

Pricing Model #2: Penetration pricing

If you want to compete on price, then price your products/services lower than market value. Increasing prices as you get more demand. (But, as Seth Godin says, "the problem with the race to the bottom is you just might win."[67])

Pricing Model #3: Economy Pricing

The Wal-Mart model is designed for those who can keep prices low but make up the profit margin by selling a ton of products in mass quantities.

Pricing model #4: Psychological Pricing

This strategy works with the "roundness" of your price. For example: $0.99 versus $1.00.

Some studies have shown that we prefer:

- Numbers with fewer syllables ($35.10 vs $35.82).
- Smaller, more frequent installments.
- A daily equivalent (only $4.99 per day).

- A number without the comma ($9999 vs $9,999).
- A precise number instead of a round number ($873.42 vs $820).
- Prices without the dollar sign (45 vs $45).

According to the book *Contagious* by Jonah Berger, when your price is under $100, it's best to use a percentage discount (eg. 25% off) but when your price is over $100, use an absolute value (e.g. $25 off).[68]

RISK REMOVAL/GUARANTEES

Removing risk(s) helps prospective clients feel more comfortable that you're going to stand behind your product or service.

Some guarantees include:

Guarantee Model #1: Try before you buy

You can provide people with a free, time-limited offer. LinkedIn uses this model with their Premium accounts. You can try their services for a free month, and they will remind you to unsubscribe so your credit card isn't billed the following month.

Guarantee Model #2: Freemiums

Your prospects can try out some of the basic elements for free, but if they want more options, they have to pay for it. I notice freemium models are often used with apps: Try it for free, but if you want more access, you have to pay for it.

Guarantee Model #3: Money-back guarantees

I've seen various ways brands use money-back guarantees to make prospects feel more comfortable with their investment. They include:

- A time-limited money-back guarantee (within a certain time limit.)
- A lifetime money-back guarantee (no time limit.)

- A money-back guarantee with terms: the client may return the product *only* if they prove they have completed the "homework" or submit they've completed action items.

Can you apply any of these sales strategies to your products or services?

INFOMERCIALS & THE PERSUASIVE "SCIENCE" BEHIND HOW THEY GET THEIR AUDIENCE TO BUY.

Have you ever sat through an infomercial?

About 20 minutes into the "show", you find you're reaching for your wallet because you're going to get *two* sets of widgets you never wanted in the first place. Right?

I'm fascinated by infomercials because they use a specific formula to persuade the audience to buy things they don't often need.

If you really study their process, you'll find they follow a similar pattern.

THE 10-STEP PROCESS OF AN INFOMERCIAL

Step #1: They identify the problem/pain that you may be dealing with today. (Or you may not know you have the problem yet!) (Building awareness.)

Step #2: Their story describes the specific benefits of their product/service to help solve the problems they've outlined. The content is aspirational for the viewer. They highlight "wouldn't you *love* to have the same product/service too?" (Generating interest.)

Step #3: They tackle the audience's top objections. (Addressing barriers to buy.)

Step #4: They feature enthusiastic testimonials that counter the objections and share how this product/service changed their lives. (Providing social proof.)

Step #5: The benefits and testimonials are typically repeated three times during the infomercial. They highlight various perspectives of how you are now (with the problem) versus how much easier your life could be with this product/service (the solution). This repetition builds momentum (Increasing desire.)

Step #6: They often address emotion within the context of how this product will help you. (i.e. How does that feel?)

Step #7: They build suspense and do not announce the cost until they are close to the end of the presentation. They build desire until the viewer is hooked and then announce the price (call-to-action): *"3 easy payments of $59.99!"*

Step #8: They offer bonuses to build on the perceived value of what you are buying (But wait…there's more! You don't just get two widgets you never thought you needed, you get four!)

Step #9: They offer a money-back guarantee so it provides a low barrier of entry to buy.

Step #10: *"And, if you buy within the next 5 minutes, you'll also receive…."* There can also be a bonus offer within a limited time-frame to make you feel like you'll miss out if you don't take action now. (Scarcity.)

You can also use some of these persuasive techniques to make your product/service/idea more appealing using social media. Here's how:

Step #1: Write blog posts or videos that address a specific problem or pain your target audience is having.

Step #2: In your content marketing, acknowledge or address your audience's objections or deepest fears. What prevents them from taking action?

Step #3: Provide proof that you are providing the perfect solution. Highlight the benefits and identify what makes your product/service/idea different than everyone else's.

Step #4: Include some "social proof." Testimonials work great here. How did someone else take action and your product/service/idea changed their life for the better?

Step #5: Reassure your audience that they will feel much better once they've taken action. Offer some sort of guarantee (and be sure to stand behind that guarantee) that eliminates the barrier to purchase.

Step #6: Over-deliver on the results. Knock it out of the park, and be sure to provide "through the roof" customer service both online and offline.

Step #7: When you follow up with your client to inquire how they are doing, for positive feedback, ask them, *"can I quote you on that?"* or *"can I use this testimonial as a part of my marketing program?"*, or *"can I uses this testimonial on my LinkedIn profile?"* For negative feedback, take action to make things right.

When they are giving you great feedback, you may also wish to ask, *"do you know anyone else who might benefit as well?"* so that you can build a network of referrals. (Perhaps even ask them to introduce you to that person on LinkedIn!)

The next time you watch an infomercial, see if you can identify the pattern listed above, and see where you can apply the same principles to your business. If the Sham-Wow guy could do it, so can you!

EXERCISE #18: IDENTIFY SALES TRIGGERS

TIME COMMITMENT: 1+ HOURS

Whether you're selling a product, a service, or your ideas, your goal is to have someone take action. By identifying various triggers, addressing the fears, and lowering the barrier to entry, your target audience is much more likely to comply.

This exercise will help you to build trust, and also help you to develop strategic content.

Think about at least three sales triggers and/or three ways to influence your ideal client and the tactics you will use.

For example:

Sales trigger:

LinkedIn announces your connection Karen has just received a job promotion to Vice President.

Tactics to build influence:

- Send Karen a handwritten "congratulations" card in the mail.
- Follow up a week later with an email to say *"Hi Karen, I hope you're settling in to your new role as Vice President (does your office have a great view?) I've closed an article I think you'll find useful. Particularly point #3 that states "_____." I'd love to take you out for lunch to celebrate your success. How does next Tuesday work for you?"*
- Introduce Karen to someone in your network that may help her in her new role.
- Ask Karen if she'd like to take a "test drive" of one of your premium products for a limited time.

It's important that these tactics be seamless and not "forced." You'll have to determine how busy Karen is and whether or not she's receptive to deepening your relationship.

HOW THE DECISION-MAKER MINDSET WORKS WITH SOCIAL MEDIA

Did you know:

- 84% of C-level/vice president (VP) executives use social media to make purchasing decisions?[69]
- Social networks, like LinkedIn, are the #1 influencer in the final stage of the purchase process?[69]
- The average B2B buyer, who uses social media for their purchase decision, is senior, has a larger budget and has a greater span of buying control than a decision maker who does not use social media?[69]
- B2B buyers find the greatest benefit of social media is gaining greater confidence in and comfort with their decision?[69]

Now it's your turn.

Write down at least three triggers and three ways you can align various tactics and strategies you can set in motion.

Sales trigger:
1. _____
_____
_____
2. _____
_____
_____
3. _____
_____
_____

Tactics to build influence:

1. _____
_____
_____

2. _____
_____
_____

3. _____
_____
_____

LESSON #19

TEACH THEM SOMETHING THEY DON'T KNOW

"Challengers know they're on the right track when they hear their customer say, 'Huh. I never thought of it that way before.'[70]*"*

~The Challenger Sale

The Challenger Sale is a book by Matthew Dixon and Brent Adamson. It states that high sales performers should be pushing prospective clients beyond their comfort zone because this approach is the most successful.

Specifically, the Challenger approach includes constructive confrontation. The goal is to present new ideas to your prospects to help solve problems they probably didn't even know they had.

Often, your target audience can Google solutions to their problems and one of your biggest competitors is actually the status quo. To get your audience motivated to make a change, you have to provide them a new perspective.

There are six traits that distinguish "challengers" from the other sales profile types:

- They offer a unique perspective to the customer/client.
- They have strong 2-way communication skills.
- They know the individual customer's/client's value drivers.
- They can identify economic drivers of their customer's/client's business.
- They are comfortable discussing money.
- They can pressure the customer/client.

Once you've challenged their assumptions, the next step is to show the prospective client quantifiable proof that you can solve their problem and provide them with a new way they should be thinking about their business.

Challenger reps must be willing to create tension and focus on value instead of price.

I'm not a natural Challenger. I prefer to make people feel comfortable instead of pushing them outside of their comfort zone. (According to the book, I'm less likely to be a successful salesperson than the Challenger-type). I wanted to ensure I shared this approach because this concept challenged my thinking about sales. I don't think I'll change into a "Challenger" overnight, but I do think it's helpful for you to find different ways you can gently push your prospective clients and get them to say "*huh. I never thought of it that way before.*"

EXERCISE #19: BREAKING OUT OF THE COMFORT ZONE

TIME COMMITMENT: 20+ MINUTES.

List at least one way you can gently challenge your target audience so they feel outside their "comfort zone." Can you provide insights that your target audience would truly be surprised to know? Can you build excitement that will add drama to the story? Make sure you can back up your insights with data or proof.

_____

_____

_____

_____

_____

_____

_____

_____

_____

_____

_____

_____

_____

_____

_____

_____

_____

_____

_____

_____

LESSON #20

DESIGN SEDUCTIVE INBOUND LEAD MAGNETS

"Heck yes! I'd vote for you".
~Napoleon Dynamite

One of the best ways to capture email addresses is through a "lead magnet." A lead magnet is an incentive that you provide for free, in exchange for obtaining contact information such as their name, email address, contact information, etc.

What makes lead magnets so powerful is that your prospects can pre-qualify themselves and actively "raise their hand" to receive more information.

Typically, when your prospects opt-in to receive information, you can also add them to your e-newsletter list. (Be sure to check out all the legal requirements about opt-ins and newsletter registration.)

One brand who has a very creative lead magnet system is Amy Porterfield (amyporterfield.com). Each week in Amy's podcasts, she offers a "freebie" which is typically a checklist or a "swipe file" that complements the content she is discussing that week. Listeners can access the freebie by visiting her website, or she lets the listener know they can text a specific number to download the content. She then uses the opportunity of the lead magnet to capture the email address and add that person to her mailing list.

Similarly, I absolutely adore Marie Forleo (marieforleo.com) who sends a free weekly video blog to help her target audience solve a specific problem. Marie calls these videos "Q & A Tuesday". (While Marie has hundreds of thousands of subscribers to her weekly videos, I swear her messages are directed at me every week.)

One lead magnet that Marie uses is "free audio training." Her call to action is: "Download this free audio training and get the clarity and confidence to build your dreams, on your terms."

Marie's target audience is predominantly made up of female entrepreneurs. She has a signature 8-week training program called B-School. The investment is $2,000 U.S.

Some of the key strategies that have helped Marie to become a multi-millionaire include:

- Building a substantial list of followers (I would guess it's in the hundreds of thousands range.)
- Deploying a weekly video that provides great solutions and inspiration, along with bloopers or showing how much fun she has producing the content (the content is extremely relevant to her target audience.)
- Offering a conditional money-back guarantee (you have to complete and submit some of the homework.)
- Providing lifetime access to the B-School material along with access to Marie via a weekly call-in class.

Be mindful that Marie and Amy have a team who help them create and deploy their programs, but they've also been marketers for a long time. One thing you'll have to also recognize as a brand, is that everyone at some point started somewhere.

COMPARISON IS A KILLER

Every single successful person started somewhere and built their network one person at a time.

Create your unique lead magnet that makes your target audience feel they *need* to have the free content you are offering.

As you create your lead magnet, think about the following steps:

Step #1: Identify your prospect's need to solve to a specific problem.

Maybe they are challenged with:
- Time-management.
- Not enough help/support.
- Needing to make more money and want to convert higher-paying clients.
- Wanting to obtain more attention through word-of-mouth.
- Issues surrounding customer service.

Step #2: Find a format or material that works best for *them*.

You'll want to reach them in the easiest way possible. What format will work best? Double check the user experience and test how it works through desktop, laptop and mobile.
- Audio
- Video
- Visual
- Copy

Step #3: Provide something of *value*.

Can you provide a "silver bullet" solution that makes one big promise to produce tangible results?
- Free Report or Whitepaper
- Free Training
- E-book (or chapter of e-book)
- Infographic
- Resource list
- "Cheat sheet"

Step #4: Follow up and stay in touch.

Did the solution help?
How could you be more of service to them?

Tools you can use for lead magnets:

- Landing page on your website.
- MailChimp (A free mail program for up to 2,000 subscribers.)
- I love MailChimp, and use a pop up on www.punchmedia.ca to provide a time management checklist.
- Hubspot

There are more expensive options out there, complete systems for larger businesses.

EXERCISE #20: CREATE/DESIGN AT LEAST ONE LEAD MAGNET

TIME COMMITMENT: 3+ HOURS FOR COPY AND DEVELOPMENT

Can you repurpose any of your existing training, copy, or material into a strong and compelling Lead Magnet? Think about one of the biggest frustrations or challenges your target audience has, and provide content that can help them solve it.

Your target audience's problem:

_____

_____

_____

Your solution:

_____

_____

_____

How it will be delivered:

_____

_____

_____

Have you done a quality assurance test?

_____

_____

_____

How you will follow up:

_____

_____

_____

_____

_____

_____

_____

LESSON #21

HOW TO OVERCOME SALES OBJECTIONS AND CLOSE THE DEAL

"I feel comfortable using legal jargon in everyday life.
(Someone whistles)
I object!"
~Legally Blonde

As we've already acknowledged, one of the most common reasons people don't change to a new service or product is because they are comfortable with the status quo. Some other objections from your target audience may be lack of budget, need to check with other decision-makers, or "it's not the right time."

To get them to take action, you may need to apply some of the following gentle persuasion "sales" techniques.

ASSUME THE SALE

Have a positive attitude that you know your idea, product, or service is a perfect fit for what they need.

Just be in a positive mindset that your audience will accept your perspective. (Refer to Lesson #2 if you need any reminders about your value.)

MAKE YOUR OFFER EXTREMELY IRRESISTIBLE

As Dean Jackson outlines in the Breakthrough DNA Report for the *I Love Marketing* podcast, when you offer someone a plate of freshly baked cookies[71], who in their right mind would say "no"?

> *"I often use an example of bringing you into my home, sitting you down in the living room, and saying "If there's anything you want to eat or drink, there's lots of stuff in the fridge...just feel free to help yourself. I'll be in the other room, if you need anything just holler"*
>
> *Again, I would be completely sincere in that offer, and I would love it if you would feel comfortable enough to help yourself to something in the fridge.... but I know that's not what you would do.*
>
> *You would feel uncomfortable imposing like that. It's the way we're raised.*
>
> *Now contrast that with me coming into the living room with a plate of freshly baked cookies, holding them right in front of you and saying "would you like a cookie?"*
>
> *The truth is, it would be very difficult for you not to take a cookie under those circumstances - even if they weren't your favorite cookie - because I've clearly gone out of my way to make these cookies for you, and it would be rude to reject me.*
>
> *Understanding that dynamic helps you realize that people are silently begging to be led."*

Mmmmm......cookies.

Sometimes being ready with various objections and counter-arguments can help to continue the dialogue.

COMMON OBJECTIONS

Here are four common objections and "at-the-ready" to help close the deal:

Objection #1: "It costs too much."

Ask *"why do you think so?"* Then, focus on the value of your offering. Break down the cost into smaller amounts and assign a financial value to each subsection. Document how long it takes for you to complete each task to provide the framework as to why you charge what you do.

Objection #2: "Things are fine the way they are right now."

Circle back to the chapter on The Challenger Sale.
What will they miss out on if they don't take action now?
What data can you provide that gets them motivated to make a change?
Provide testimonials from people who changed to your product/service and how much better they are for having done so.

Objection #3: "I'm too busy right now."

Acknowledge that you don't want to waste their time and you understand what it's like to be busy. Ask for a suitable time you can call them back, or simply dig in and say, *"if I could show you a proven system that would help you (insert what you deliver here), is that something you would invest five minutes to talk about?"*

Objection #4: "I need to run this by the decision-maker."

Find out (ideally as early in the process as possible) who the decision-maker is and try to bring them into the process with a joint sales meeting. Proactively connect with the decision-maker on LinkedIn and do your best to educate them throughout the process (without being a pest and "ccing" them on every correspondence.)

Provide your prospect with common objections and how your brand is different than everyone else.

When trying to "close a sale," be sure to follow up regularly with "gentle reminders." Sometimes when I get busy, it's helpful if the salesperson follows up with me via email or phone to remind me to take action. I don't consider them a pest, in fact I like being reminded that I have to take action!

EXERCISE #21: IDENTIFY BARRIERS TO CLOSE AND HAVE YOUR ANSWER READY!

TIME COMMITMENT: 10 MINUTES.

You may come across the same barriers over and over again. Apply some of the above techniques and principles of persuasion to get your prospect to say *yes*!

List at least one common objection, and how you'll address it.

Objection:

_____

_____

_____

_____

_____

How you will respond:

_____

_____

_____

_____

_____

_____

_____

_____

_____

_____

_____

_____

_____

_____

_____

_____

LESSON #22

AFTER THE SALE IS WHERE THE FUN BEGINS

"Louie, I think this is the beginning of a beautiful friendship."

~Casablanca

While this lesson doesn't specifically address social media, it's exceptionally important to ensure you are building relationships from a holistic perspective. Most people think that the sale is the end of the relationship, when in fact – from your client's perspective – it's just the beginning.

Did you know, that while 80% of companies *say* they deliver "superior" service, but only 8% clients say that companies *actually* deliver "superior" customer service![72]

According to many statistics, including a report by Bain & Company, it's much cheaper to keep your current clients happy than it is to convert new ones.

> *"In financial services, for example, a 5% increase in customer retention produces more than a 25% increase in profit. Why? Return customers tend to buy more from a company over time. As they do, your operating costs to serve them decline. What's more, return customers refer others to your company. And they'll often pay a premium to continue to do business with you rather than switch to a competitor with whom they're neither familiar nor comfortable."* [74]

A report by White House Office of Consumer Affairs' Return on Behavior magazine stated that loyal customers are worth up to 10 times as much as their first purchase. [75]

So the question is: **What are you going to do to make their experience *remarkable*?**

As a marketer, I'm keenly aware when I receive an "over the top" experience. Often, these experiences are found in the most unusual places, such as my periodontist, Dr. Hoffman. You wouldn't think an experience at the periodontist would be a delightful lesson in customer/patient experience, would you?

Some key insights I noticed:

- **Key insight #1:** Dr. Hoffman is exceptional with his time-management. He knows how to make his patients feel very important with his one-on-one interaction, but he also appears to be very mindful of always being on-time.
- **Key insight #2:** During our consultation, Dr. Hoffman was very thorough with his explanation of the problem(s) and provided clear solutions as to his approach.
- **Key insight #3:** While he was waiting for X-rays to be processed and had to leave the room for a moment, he provided me with a binder of testimonials – just to reassure me that I was making the right decision to trust him.

- **Key insight #4:** I was reminded about my upcoming appointment by email (at the time, no other practices were using this as an option). I loved that I was contacted in a way that I could confirm with them my appointment without having to call them.
- **Key insight #5:** After the procedure, Dr. Hoffman called me personally at home – after hours. He did not delegate this to an assistant or hygienist. He wanted to be sure there weren't any complications after the fact.

All of these touchpoints ensured I felt like I was an important patient who he genuinely cared about. I also know other patients of Dr. Hoffman and he consistently provides this same level of concern and care for all his patients. (Big shout out to everyone on his team who are a big part of why his practice runs so smoothly.)

Here are some other ideas on ways you can over-deliver:

- Write a personalized and handwritten thank you card.
- Follow up with a video that includes additional free tips or "hacks."
- Send a small gift (a book, gift card, flowers.)
- Take clients out for lunch or coffee after the sale.
- Donate to a charity in their name.
- Provide them with an additional bonus of your products/services at no charge.
- Reach out and congratulate them on any special events or celebrations within their business.
- Wish them a Happy Birthday or Happy (work) Anniversary.

Don't be "meh," be remarkable.

EXERCISE #22: WRITE DOWN TWO WAYS YOU CAN OVER-DELIVER

TIME COMMITMENT: 5 MINUTES

LESSON #23

REFERRALS: THE NEXT GENERATION

"Merely satisfying customers will not be enough to earn their loyalty. Instead, they must experience exceptional service worthy of their repeat business and referral. Understand the factors that drive this customer revolution."

~Rick Tate

As we've discussed, word-of-mouth is your *best* source of marketing. In fact, 90% of people trust referrals from people they know and 70% trusted consumer opinions posted online.[75] (Gotta love that "social proof"!)

So how do you get your happy clients to share word-of-mouth awareness about you and your business?

Ask them straight out:

> *"Alex, if we meet or exceed your expectations within the first few months, would you introduce us to three people who could benefit from our services?"*

Follow up with phone calls and/or email. The day of or the day after, a week later and one month after the sale.

> *"How is our product/service working? Is it measuring up to your expectations?"* If they say yes, ask *"is there someone else in your network who could benefit from the same kind of results you've been having?"*

Go to LinkedIn and look at your client's connections. Choose specific people who fit your Ideal Client Avatar and ask your client to introduce you to them.

Provide happy clients with a specific link and ask them to provide you with a review or testimonial on the most appropriate social media channel(s) (Google, Facebook, etc.)

Act on your feedback. If your clients have mentioned how happy they are with you, ask:

> *"Can I quote you on this? We love to highlight our clients who are happy with their results."*

Write down what they've said, send it to your client for their approval and use it on your marketing material, you also may wish to reach out and ask your client to include this testimonial on your LinkedIn profile.

EXERCISE #23: REFERRALS: WHO YOU GONNA CALL?

TIME COMMITMENT: 1+ HOURS

Make a list of five potential referrals and how you will ask them to introduce you to your that connection.

> Pro Tip: LinkedIn is an excellent resource for mutual introductions!

Don't feel comfortable asking for a referral? Think about the last time you received great customer service. Did you voluntarily give them feedback they could use for their marketing material? Would you have given it to them if they had asked?

If you don't ask, you won't get. Reach out now to five people who can help you "spread the word."

1. _____
   _____
2. _____
   _____
3. _____
   _____
4. _____
   _____
5. _____

LESSON #24

EMPOWER INFLUENCERS TO BE YOUR UNPAID SALES FORCE!

"You're my ambassador of quawn, man"

~Jerry Maguire

Just like asking for referrals, you can also leverage influencers to share news about you as well. Influencers are people who help to spread word-of-mouth awareness. They can range from your next door neighbor to a famous celebrity. Influencers have been referred to as "raving fans" or "brand ambassadors."

One key factor that makes influencers different than anyone else is that people listen to their opinion and are more likely to take action (or avoid taking action) based on the influencers' feedback.

I'd like to introduce to you my friend Dottie, who (I think) is the Brand Ambassador of Anna Maria Island.

THE BRAND AMBASSADOR OF ANNA MARIA ISLAND

Every year our family visits this little island in Florida nestled between Sarasota and Tampa called Anna Maria Island.

The first year we stayed in this tropical paradise, we met Dottie Mizzi who lives in the complex we were renting. Dottie and her husband George, retired here about a decade ago and they are now year-round residents there.

It seems *everyone* on Anna Maria Island knows Dottie. She's involved in charity work, and she organizes many local events. Dottie is very connected and involved with her a large network of friends (many of whom live all over the world.) She regularly stays in touch with both the locals, and those of us who visit the island every year.

Every year when we return to Anna Maria Island, we typically start our conversation with, *"So Dottie, what's new here on the Island? Any new shops? How are the new restaurants?"*

We trust that Dottie will give us the *real* story about the quality and value of every new restaurant or shop. Dottie likes to be "in the know," and will gladly give us all the details of her experience. She gives us her honest recommendations about to where to go, or the shops and restaurants we should avoid.

To me, Dottie is the unofficial "Brand Ambassador of Anna Maria Island".

Dottie's opinion matters to her network. Anna Maria Island is predominantly a tourist town where the same people return year after year. We rely on Dottie to vet all the good spots for us, and we all trust her judgement.

Why test out something new, when Dottie has done all the research for us?

You probably know a "Dottie"; someone who is "in the know" and "on the go." Someone who is very connected in her local community, and happily shares her "two cents" about where to go (or where to avoid).

If local establishments were smart, they would court Dottie to become their VIP. For example, restaurants should invite Dottie to their Grand Opening and invite her to see the kitchen. They should listen to her opinions about what she likes and ensure she's given the best customer service possible. These restaurant and shops could provide her with marketing material so she can distribute the information to new people to the island. If I were the shop or restaurant, I'd tailor some marketing material with a free coupon that included "complimentary dessert/product courtesy of Dottie Mizzi."

According to the book *Anatomy of Buzz*[76] by Emanuel Rosen, you can identify your influencers using the acronym A.C.T.I.V.E:

- **Ahead in adoption:** They aren't necessarily the first to adopt new products, but they ahead of most of us. (Think of the people who line up for days for the new Apple product or Star Wars film. These people always want to be the first in line to experience the launch and want the "bragging rights" to have first access.)
- **Connected:** Within a specific clique, these people are hungry for information and want to share their experiences with others.
- **Travelers:** Some people travel physically, other people "travel virtually." They attend meetings or are active in an online community.
- **Information-hungry:** These influencers want to be considered experts within their niche.
- **Vocal:** One thing you can count on, these influencers are opinionated and want others to now about their opinions.
- **Exposed to the media more than others:** Similar to "information-hungry," these people read a lot more than others do.

You may not even recognize these influencers at first. They may be currently providing you with feedback on your social media channels. You may find they are the key people who share your posts with their network.

Sometimes these influencers can even come in the form of a follower who is complaining. As long as they aren't overt trolls and genuinely want to help you to improve your client experience, when you transform their negative experience into a positive one, they'll tell anyone who will listen.

You may have already heard this, but people who have a good experience tell an average of nine people. Those who have had a negative experience tell 16 people.[77] On social media, this reach is amplified exponentially.

It's important to over-deliver each and every time.

Other important statistics to note:

- 90% of consumers who recalled reading online reviews claimed that positive reviews influenced their decision to buy.[78]
- 86% said that negative reviews had also influenced buying decisions.[79]
- Brand advocates are 70% more likely to be seen as a good source of information by people around them.[80]

Influencers can be:

- Happy employees
- Suppliers
- Current clients
- Journalists
- Bloggers
- Industry experts
- Strangers who post reviews

In traditional media, Oprah Winfrey was probably one of the most well-known influencers. Her millions of followers would eagerly go out and purchase the products she endorsed on her show. Her influence was so powerful, the term "The Oprah Effect" was coined, because many companies would generate up to 1,000%[81] growth shortly after they were mentioned on her show.

Your influencers don't need to be as famous as Oprah. As long as they drive action and not just awareness, these brand ambassadors essentially act as your unpaid salespeople.

YOUR ONLINE CIRCLE OF INFLUENCE

In 2016, there are 3.4 billion internet users, and 2.3 billion users of social media.[82]

For a moment, think about how many people you could connect by posting on all your social media channels:

- What is your total potential reach within your 1st degree connections?
- How many 2nd degree eyeballs can you reach if you're able to get your 1st degree connections to engage?
- Think about your key influencers. How many people can THEY reach?

Empowering your circle of influence to share your content is really important because their endorsement can lead to a 3x to 10x increase in conversions.[83]

TOP WAYS YOU CAN NURTURE RELATIONSHIPS WITH INFLUENCERS

- Always lead with your integrity. Be honest, be transparent, and be of service.
- Reach them early, give them "insider secrets" and exclusive offers before everyone else.
- Ask for their opinion, address their concerns and make changes (if appropriate.)
- Always over deliver.
- Give them credit and kudos. Make them the "hero" of the story. Can you highlight them as a case study?

EXERCISE #24: CREATE YOUR INFLUENCER LIST

TIME COMMITMENT: 40+ MINUTES

Create a list of influencers you *want* to be connected to.

Step #1: Create a list of at least 10 people you are connected to who could help share your message (and yes, you can include your Mom).

Step #2: Identify the channel(s) where they share their messages. Online? In person?

Step #3: What information will you provide them with?

Step #4: How have you made it easy for them to share?

Step #5: What plan of action or correspondence do you have to get them to share?

LESSON #25

IF YOU LIKE IT, THEN YOU SHOULD PUT A RING ON IT: ENGAGEMENT AND VIRAL MARKETING

"Once an idea has taken hold of the brain it's almost impossible to eradicate. An idea that is fully formed — fully understood — that sticks right in there somewhere."

~Inception

The cacophony of social media can make it more challenging to have your message heard. And the "noise" is also making it getting harder and harder to get engagement (some channels have higher engagement than others.)

Did you know that[84]:

- On Facebook users "like" 4,166,667 posts every minute, which adds up to 250 million posts per hour?
- Twitter users generate 347,222 tweets each minute – or 21 million tweets per hour?
- YouTube sees over 3 billion video views per day and every minute, over 300 hours of new video is uploaded to the platform by its users?

Whew! That's enough to make anyone's head spin.

And while we know that there are 2.5 quintillion bytes of data[85] being created each day, less than 1% of the online population is creating new content.[86]

As you learned in Lesson #10, you have a huge opportunity to dominate through thought leadership by posting the right content, in the right context.

Compelling, emotional content is more likely to go "viral" but to have something actually go "viral" is almost impossible.

You may not be the next *Gangnam Style*, but there are key ways you can make your messages more engaging and "shareable":

- Ask you audience for their opinion. Encourage the reader to contribute their feedback.
- Simply ask them to share. You don't want to do this for every post, but once in a while, actually telling your reader to share the post will make them take action.
- Make sure your website has easy-to-access social media buttons that the reader can click to share.
- Pay to have your content "boosted" through native advertising. Be sure to choose the right message to the right audience.

A few years ago, I came across a Facebook page for a charity called "The Girl Effect". I loved how their online marketing material provided a complete downloadable toolkit, in a PDF format, that would allow anyone to promote their charity.

This kit included turnkey templates that allowed people to buy standard sized iron-on transfers to t-shirts, stickers, envelopes, cards etc. It provided printable posters and FAQ sheets so people could post information about this charity in their office kitchens, or other bulletin boards.

Make your brand message easy-to-share. Provide a strong call-to-action, and people may just help to promote you!

EXERCISE #25: LIST AT LEAST ONE WAY YOU'LL MAKE YOUR MESSAGES EASY-TO-SHARE

TIME COMMITMENT: 5 MINUTES.

DEEP THOUGHTS ABOUT CONVERTING YOUR TARGET AUDIENCE

Conversion may work in the alliteration of the title of this book, but as I'm sure you've recognized, sales isn't about pushing or giving someone something they don't want.

Conversion, is about a "win-win" situation, where each person benefits from the exchange of products, services or information.

Author and sales trainer, Jeffrey Gitomer said *"If a prospect says, 'I'm not interested,' it really means that you are not interesting. They are **not** engaged.*[87]

You're not necessarily selling; you're educating. You're creating thought leadership. You're developing a holistic approach to creating awareness from new prospective high-quality leads while also nurturing the deep connections you've already established.

No one is ever going to buy something they don't need.

Sometimes your target audience needs a little gentle nudge. Sometimes they need reassurances that they are making the right decision.

Find ways to make your brand appealing. Provide "win-win" opportunities that your brand ambassadors can use to make them feel powerful about their authority.

Your messages are important. You just have to find the right audience who is receptive to your vision.

POST-SCRIPT

"You have brains in your head.
You have feet in your shoes.
You can steer yourself any direction you choose.
You're on your own. And you know what you know.
And YOU are the one who'll decide where to go..."

Dr. Seuss, Oh, The Places You'll Go

So there you have it folks. **You are a brand.** You have the power to create a strong presence, connect with quality people, and convert higher-paying clients using social media.

As a strategist, I know that there is no silver bullet to obtaining success. One size does not fit all. You have to continuously set goals, and take action to obtain success. Try new approaches; test, rinse, repeat.

Some days you'll wake up and feel "not good enough". Other days you'll find you're kicking ass and taking names.

As Dr. Maya Angelou said, *"Do the best you can until you know better. Then when you know better, do better."*

Did you go through and compete all the lessons? If not, *why* not?

What is holding you back from stepping into your greatness?
What excuses are you using?
- I don't have enough time.
- I don't have enough resources.
- I'm still not ready.

If you still have doubts about launching now, you may want to check out Steven Pressfield's book *The War of Art*, which does a deep dive into resistance:

"Resistance will tell you anything to keep you from doing your work. It will perjure, fabricate, falsify; seduce, bully, cajole. Resistance is protean. It will assume any form, if that's what it takes to deceive you. It will reason with you like a lawyer or jam a nine-millimeter in your face like a stickup man. Resistance has no conscience. It will pledge anything to get a deal, then double-cross you as soon as your back is turned. If you take Resistance at its word, you deserve everything you get. Resistance is always lying and always full of shit.[90]*"*

Everyone struggles with resistance and procrastination. These feeling are fueled by fear:
- Fear of failure.
- Fear of success.
- Fear of not being enough.

In her book *Return To Love*, Marianne Williamson[89] says:

"Our deepest fear is not that we are inadequate. Our deepest fear is that we are powerful beyond measure. It is our light, not our darkness that most frightens us. We ask ourselves, Who am I to be brilliant, gorgeous, talented, and fabulous? Actually, who are you not to be? You are a child of God. Your playing small does not serve the world. There is nothing enlightened about shrinking so that other people will not feel insecure around you. We are all meant to shine, as children do. We were born to make manifest the glory of God that is within us. It is not just in some of us; it is in everyone and as we let our own light shine, we unconsciously give others permission to do the same. As we are liberated from our own fear, our presence automatically liberates others."

Remember, the world needs you! You have specialized knowledge that no one else knows about. There isn't a single person in the universe who holds the keys to the information you have.

You owe it to your target audience, and you owe it to yourself, to step into your power and own your brand.

I've given you the strategy, and the lessons, and the info. Now it's up to you to launch.

Be brave—Change the world.
I believe in you.

YOUR PLAN OF ACTION CHECKLIST

CREATE		
WHAT YOU'RE GOING TO DO	**WHEN YOU'RE GOING TO DO IT**	**MARK WHEN IT'S COMPLETE**
Define your core values		
Set your specific goals and objectives		
Construct your unique value proposition		
Reframe negative feedback		
Plan for the worst-case scenario		
Audit your online impression		
Create your ideal client avatar blueprint		
Construct your ideal client's story		
Set up/improve your LinkedIn profile (Include a professional photo, update your headline, craft your Summary)		
Get testimonials		
Write 5 blog posts		
Map out your schedule for when you will post		

CONNECT

WHAT YOU'RE GOING TO DO	WHEN YOU'RE GOING TO DO IT	MARK WHEN IT'S COMPLETE
Reach out to 5 connections each week		
Connect with _____ new people each week		
Introduce _____ new people each week		
Map out your prospects path to purchase. (Map their touch-point and add the strategy. Make the strategic changes to your marketing.)		

CONVERT

WHAT YOU'RE GOING TO DO	WHEN YOU'RE GOING TO DO IT	MARK WHEN IT'S COMPLETE
Identify five conversion tactics you can take to guide your prospect		
Reframe your feelings about selling		
Identify at least three sales triggers and/or way to influence your ideal client		
What's one way you can challenge your target audience to push outside their comfort zone?		
Create at least one lead magnet		

CONVERT

WHAT YOU'RE GOING TO DO	WHEN YOU'RE GOING TO DO IT	MARK WHEN IT'S COMPLETE
Identify objections and have your answer ready!		
List two ways you can over-deliver.		
List 10 people who could refer you. (When will you reach out to them?)		
List 10 potential influencers When will you reach out to them?		
What information will you send to these influencers? Is the content easy to share?		

LINKEDIN CHECKLIST

#1: CREATE

- ❑ Professional photo
- ❑ Strong headline
- ❑ Summary
- ❑ Current Position
- ❑ Past Positions
- ❑ Use of strong keywords
- ❑ Customized URL
- ❑ Education
- ❑ Projects, Publications, Awards etc.
- ❑ Focus on top 10 skills
- ❑ Add multimedia

#2: CONNECT

- ❑ Connect with at least 50 people (personalize connection requests)
- ❑ Follow your Company Page

#3: CONVERSE & CONVERT

- ❑ Re-share your Company's status updates with your network
- ❑ Share relevant articles privately with specific connections

END NOTES

MODULE #1: CREATE

1. https://en.wikipedia.org/wiki/Facebook
2. newsroom.fb.com/company-info
3. https://en.wikipedia.org/wiki/Prosumer
4. Godin, Seth (1999). Permission Marketing: Turning Strangers Into Friends And Friends Into Customers.
5. Peters, Tom. (1997, August). The Brand Called You. Fast Company, Retrieved from https://www.fastcompany.com/28905/brand-called-you

LESSON #1: WHO ARE YOU?

6. https://en.wikiquote.org/wiki/Blaise_Pascal
7. Sinek, Simon (2009). Start With Why
8. Fell, Jason (2013, December). The 10 Most Overused Buzzwords on LinkedIn. Entrepreneur, Retrieved from https://www.entrepreneur.com/article/225165

LESSON #2: WHAT IS THE ROI OF YOU?

9. http://www.investopedia.com/terms/r/returnoninvestment.asp

10. Port, Michael (2010). Book Yourself Solid.
11. https://en.wikiquote.org/wiki/Maya_Angelou
12. https://business.linkedin.com/sales-solutions/blog/migrated/s/sales-managers-are-you-using-these-metrics-to-measure-social-selling-performance
13. www.brandyourself.com

LESSON #4: FACING YOUR FEAR OF PUTTING YOURSELF "OUT THERE"

14. http://www.youtube.com/watch?v=iCvmsMzlF7o
15. Koren, Leonard (1994). Wabi-Sabi for Artists, Designers, Poets and Philosophers. Stone Bridge Press.
16. Cash, Johnny (1993) Academy of Acheivement. Retreived from http://www.achievement.org
17. http://www.theodore-roosevelt.com/trsorbonnespeech.html

LESSON #5: WHAT IF SOMEONE SAYS SOMETHING BAD? THE LESSONS I LEARNED ABOUT PUBLIC RELATIONS 101.

18. http://laws-lois.justice.gc.ca/eng/acts/C-46/section-403-20100108.html

LESSON #7: HOW WELL DO YOU KNOW YOUR IDEAL CLIENT?

19. Manage The Cross-Touchpoint Customer Journey (2014). Retreived from https://www.forrester.com/report/Manage+The+CrossTouchpoint+Customer+Journey/-/E-RES86761
20. https://www.thinkwithgoogle.com/collections/zero-moment-truth.html
21. http://www.vcloudnews.com/every-day-big-data-statistics-2-5-quintillion-bytes-of-data-created-daily/

LESSON #9: CREATE YOUR PROFESSIONAL PRESENCE USING LINKEDIN

22. Ambron, Patrick (2012) Want to Look Better in Google? Our Data Shows You the Best Ways [our first infographic]. Retreived from http://blog.brandyourself.com/
23. Boutin, Chad (2006) Snap judgments decide a face's character, psychologist finds. Retreived from https://www.princeton.edu

24. Corliss, Rebecca (2012) LinkedIn 277% More Effective for Lead Generation Than Facebook & Twitter [New Data]. Retreived from http://blog.hubspot.com/
25. 2104 State of B2B Procurement Study: Uncovering the Shifting Landscape in B2B Commerce. Retreived from https://www.accenture.com/t20150624T211502__w__/us-en/_acnmedia/Accenture/Conversion-Assets/DotCom/Documents/Global/PDF/Industries_15/Accenture-B2B-Procurement-Study.pdf
26. https://www.linkedin.com/static?key=pop%2Fpop_more_profile_completeness
27. Wargo, Eric (2006, July) Observer "How Many Seconds to a First Impression?". Retrieved from http://www.psychologicalscience.org

LESSON #10: GET "SOCIAL PROOF" VIA TESTIMONIALS

28. Cialdini, Robert (2009). Influence: The Psychology of Persuasion.
29. Schulze, Holger (2013). B2B Content Marketing Trends. Retrieved from http://www.slideshare.net/hschulze/b2b-content-marketing-trends-2013/6-B2B_CONTENT_MARKETING_TRENDS_Read
30. Anderson, Myles (2014) 88% Of Consumers Trust Online Reviews As Much As Personal Recommendations. Search Engine Land. Retrieved from http://searchengineland.com.
31. http://www.searchquotes.com/quotation/The_more_facts_you_tell,_the_more_you_sell._An_advertisement%27s_chance_for_success_invariably_increas/218131/

LESSON #11: CREATE THOUGHT LEADERSHIP AND DOMINATE YOUR NICHE

32. Sinek, Simon (2013, February). Simon Sinek: How great leaders inspire action. Retrieved from https://www.ted.com/talks/simon_sinek_how_great_leaders_inspire_action?language=en
33. Schwartz, Julie (2012) The Six Pillars of a Successful Thought Leadership Strategy. Retreived from http://www.itsma.com/six-pillars-of-a-successful-thought-leadership-strategy/
34. LinkedIn Sales Solutions. How to guide to Social Selling. Retrieved from https://business.linkedin.com/content/dam/business/sales-solutions/global/en_US/site/pdf/ebooks/how-to-guide-to-social-selling-ebook.pdf

35. Miller, Jason. Introducing the 2016 Sophisticated Marketer's Guide to Thought Leadership. Retrieved from https://business.linkedin.com/marketing-solutions/blog/best-practices--thought-leadership/2016/introducing-the-2016-sophisticated-marketers-guide-to-thought-le

36. https://www.goodreads.com/author/quotes/25181.David_Ogilvy

37. Smith, Kelly (2016, June) 55 Easy Ways To Write A Headline That Will Reach Your Readers. Retrieved from http://coschedule.com/blog/write-a-headline/

38. Lloyd, Ian (n.d.) Why Every SEO Strategy needs Infographics. Retrieved from http://www.webmarketinggroup.co.uk/

39. Pant, Ritu (2015, January) Visual Marketing: A Picture's Worth 60,000 Words. Retrieved from http://www.business2community.com/

40. Solis, Brian (2013, February) No Business Is Too Big To Fail Or Too Small To Succeed – Sobering Stats On Business Failures. Retrieved from http://www.briansolis.com/

MODULE #2: CONNECT

41. Rouse, Margaret (n.d). Retrieved from http://searchnetworking.techtarget.com/definition/Metcalfes-Law

42. Kosner, Anthony Wing (2012, May) Facebook Values Itself Based on Metcalfe's Law, But the Market Is Using Zipf's. Retrieved from: http://www.forbes.com/sites/anthonykosner/2012/05/31/facebook-values-itself-based-on-metcalfes-law-but-the-market-is-using-zipfs/#6fc830ea6259

43. Kosner, Anthony Wing (2012, May) Facebook Values Itself Based on Metcalfe's Law, But the Market Is Using Zipf's. Retrieved from: http://www.forbes.com/sites/anthonykosner/2012/05/31/facebook-values-itself-based-on-metcalfes-law-but-the-market-is-using-zipfs/#6fc830ea6259

44. https://www.youtube.com/watch?v=mcskckuosxQ

45. Reilly, Paul (2015, May) You Don't Have To Be Different To Succeed. Retrieved from http://www.reillysalestraining.com/you-dont-have-to-be-different-to-succeed/

46. Hisaka, Alex (2015, March) Sales Managers, Are You Using These Metrics to Measure Social Selling Performance? Retrieved from https://business.linkedin.com/sales-solutions/blog/migrated/s/sales-managers-are-you-using-these-metrics-to-measure-social-selling-performance

47. Hisaka, Alex (2015, March) Sales Managers, Are You Using These Metrics to Measure Social Selling Performance? Retrieved from https://business.linkedin.com/sales-solutions/blog/migrated/s/sales-managers-are-you-using-these-metrics-to-measure-social-selling-performance

LESSON #12: ALWAYS BE COLLABORATING (AND CONNECTING)

48. LinkedIn Content Marketing Tactical Plan. Retrieved from https://business.linkedin.com/content/dam/business/marketing-solutions/global/en_US/campaigns/pdfs/linkedIn-marketing-tactical-plan-2015-v2-en-us.pdf
49. Wikipedia (n.d.). Retrieved from https://en.wikipedia.org/wiki/Neuro-linguistic_programming
50. Cialdini, Robert (2009). Influence: The Psychology of Persuasion.

LESSON #13: MAP YOUR CLIENT'S JOURNEY THROUGH MICRO-MOMENTS AND TOUCHPOINTS

51. Retail Analytics Moves To The Frontline: Benchmark 2014. Retrieved from: http://www.rsrresearch.com/research/retail-analytics-moves-to-the-frontline-benchmark-2014
52. Berger, Jonah (2013) Contagious. Why Things Catch On.

LESSON #14: MAKE NEW CONNECTIONS USING SOCIAL MEDIA

53. Hisaka, Alex (2015, March) Sales Managers, Are You Using These Metrics to Measure Social Selling Performance? Retrieved from https://business.linkedin.com/sales-solutions/blog/migrated/s/sales-managers-are-you-using-these-metrics-to-measure-social-selling-performance
54. https://press.linkedin.com/about-linkedin
55. The Sales Manager's Guide to Driving Social Media Adoption and Revenue. Retrieved from https://business.linkedin.com/content/dam/business/sales-solutions/global/en_US/c/pdfs/the-sales-managers-guide-to-driving-social-media-adoption-and-revenue-en-us.pdf
56. How Personalized Selling Unlocks Competitive Advantage. Retrieved from https://business.linkedin.com/content/dam/business/sales-solutions/global/en_US/c/pdfs/LinkedIn_LI013_EBK_CompetitiveAdvantage_FINAL_v002.pdf
57. Sexton, Koka (2013, October) How to Use a Multi-threading Approach in B2B Sales. Retrieved from https://business.linkedin.com/sales-solutions/blog/h/how-to-use-a-multi-threading-approach-in-b2b-sales)

MODULE #3: CONVERT

58. Pink, Daniel (2012) To Sell Is Human.
59. Ku, Daniel (2105) The State of Social Selling in2016 [INFOGRAPHIC]. Retreived from http://www.salesforlife.com/blog/infographics/the-state-of-social-selling-in-2016-infographic/
60. Achieving Social Selling Success. Retrieved from https://business.linkedin.com/content/dam/business/sales-solutions/global/en_US/site/pdf/ebooks/how-leading-sales-pros-use-linkedin-for-social-selling.pdf
61. Hisaka, Alex (2014, September) How B2B Buyers Perceive Sales Professionals. Retrieved from https://business.linkedin.com/sales-solutions/blog/h/how-b2b-buyers-perceive-sales-professionals
62. Hisaka, Alex (2014, September) How B2B Buyers Perceive Sales Professionals. Retrieved from https://business.linkedin.com/sales-solutions/blog/h/how-b2b-buyers-perceive-sales-professionalshttps://business.linkedin.com/content/dam/business/sales-solutions/global/en_US/site/pdf/ebooks/how-leading-sales-pros-use-linkedin-for-social-selling.pdf
63. Achieving Social Selling Success. Retrieved from https://business.linkedin.com/content/dam/business/sales-solutions/global/en_US/site/pdf/ebooks/how-leading-sales-pros-use-linkedin-for-social-selling.pdf
64. How & Why Native Ads Are Paving A Path To Greater Engagement. Retrieved from http://amobee.com/how-why-native-ads-are-paving-a-path-to-greater-engagement/

LESSON #18: SALES TRIGGERS, INFLUENCE AND WAYS YOU CAN REACH OUT

65. Getting Started with Social Selling on LinkedIn. Retrieved from https://business.linkedin.com/content/dam/me/business/en-us/sales-solutions/resources/pdfs/linkedIn-getting-started-with-social-selling-ebook.pdf
66. Nelson, Jacqueline (2011, April) Loco for Lulu. Retrieved from http://www.canadianbusiness.com/lifestyle/loco-for-lulu/
67. Godin, Seth (2012). Retrieved from http://sethgodin.typepad.com/seths_blog/2012/08/the-race-to-the-bottom.html
68. Berger, Jonah (2013) Contagious. Why Things Catch On.
69. Moran, Gerry (2015, March) 30 LinkedIn Sales Triggers. Retrieved from https://marketingthink.com/30-linkedin-social-selling-sales-triggers/

LESSON #19: TEACH THEM SOMETHING THEY DON'T KNOW

70. Dixon, Matt and Brent Adamson (2011) The Challenger Sale.

LESSON #21: HOW TO OVERCOME SALES OBJECTIONS AND CLOSE THE DEAL

71. Jackson, Dean and Joe Polish. (n.d.) Breakthrough DNA. Retrieved from https://s3.amazonaws.com/ilovemarketing/ Breakthrough%2BDNA-+FREE+REPORT.pdf

LESSON #22: AFTER THE SALE IS WHERE THE FUN BEGINS

72. 75 Customer Service Facts, Quotes and Statistics. Retrieved from https://www.helpscout.net/75-customer-service-facts-quotes-statistics/
73. Reichheld, Fred. Prescription for cutting costs. Retrieved from http://www.bain.com/Images/BB_Prescription_cutting_costs.pdf
74. 75 Customer Service Facts, Quotes and Statistics. Retrieved from https://www.helpscout.net/75-customer-service-facts-quotes-statistics/

LESSON #23: REFERRALS: THE NEXT GENERATION

75. Global Advertising Consumers Trust Real Friends and Virtual Strangers The Most (2009, July). Retrieved from http://www.nielsen.com/us/en/insights/news/2009/global-advertising-consumers-trust-real-friends-and-virtual-strangers-the-most.html

LESSON #24: EMPOWER INFLUENCERS TO BE YOUR UNPAID SALES FORCE!

76. Rosen, Emanuel (2000) The Anatomy of Buzz: How to Create Word of Mouth Marketing.
77. 75 Customer Service Facts, Quotes and Statistics. Retrieved from https://www.helpscout.net/75-customer-service-facts-quotes-statistics/
78. Gesenhues, Amy (2013, April) Survey: 90% Of Customers Say Buying Decisions Are Influenced By Online Reviews. Retrieved from http://marketingland.com/survey-customers-more-frustrated-by-how-long-it-takes-to-resolve-a-customer-service-issue-than-the-resolution-38756

79. Pinkham, Ryan (2013, April) 90% of Consumers Say Online Reviews Impact Buying Decisions ... And Other Hot Topics. Retrieved from http://blogs.constantcontact.com/do-customers-trust-online-reviews
80. Brand Advocates Share More Info (2011, March). Retrieved from http://www.marketingcharts.com/online/brand-advocates-share-more-info-17369
81. Hornbuckle, David M (n.d.) The Oprah Effect. Retrieved from http://www.inc.com/articles/2009/08/oprah.html
82. Kemp, Simon (2016, January) Digital in 2016. Retrieved from http://wearesocial.com/uk/special-reports/digital-in-2016
83. The Content Marketing Institute. The Complete Guide To Influencer Marketing: Strategies, Templates & Tools. Retrieved from http://contentmarketinginstitute.com/wp-content/uploads/2014/06/Influencer_Marketing_eBook.pdf

LESSON #25: IF YOU LIKE IT, THEN YOU SHOULD PUT A RING ON IT: ENGAGEMENT AND VIRAL MARKETING

84. We Are Social Media. (2015, August) How Much Data Is Generated Every Minute On Social Media? Retrieved from http://wersm.com/how-much-data-is-generated-every-minute-on-social-media/#ixzz4Eby0Rn1x
85. IBM. What is big data? Retrieved from https://www-01.ibm.com/software/data/bigdata/what-is-big-data.html
86. https://en.wikipedia.org/wiki/1%25_rule_(Internet_culture)
87. Is there a secret of sales? YES! But you already know it! Retrieved from http://www.gitomer.com/articles/ViewPublicArticle.html?key=ajcdMibak3PNoma1McBURw%3D%3D

POST-SCRIPT

88. Pressfield, Steven (2016) The War of Art.
89. Williamson, Marianne (2009) Return To Love

ACKNOWLEDGEMENTS

A friend is one that knows you as you are, understands where you have been, accepts what you have become, and still, gently allows you to grow."
—William Shakespeare

I consider myself to be exceptionally lucky. I'm surrounded by my best friends on a daily basis. I owe so many thanks.

To my mom, my brother, and my sister, who are my favorite people in the whole wide world.

To my life-long besties, Denise and Sara, who are always there to listen and give advice no matter if it's day or night. To all my amazing friends who have encouraged me and helped me throughout this book-writing process: Dawn Salter, Katherine Stoddart, Doris Chung, Rob Ciancamerla, Andrea Kennedy and Elizabeth Payea-Butler. To all the people who allowed me to use their real names and stories: Nate Issacson, Darren Vance, Dottie Mizzie, Terry Aldread, Anita Windisman, D/C Pallister, Alexandria Durrell, Janet Kelly and Sue Horner.

And most importantly, I dedicate this book to the love of my life, Brady, who is my muse and my soul.

**"No one else will ever know
the strength of my love for you.
After all, you're the only one who
knows the sound of my heart
from the inside."**

—Kristen Proby, Fight with Me